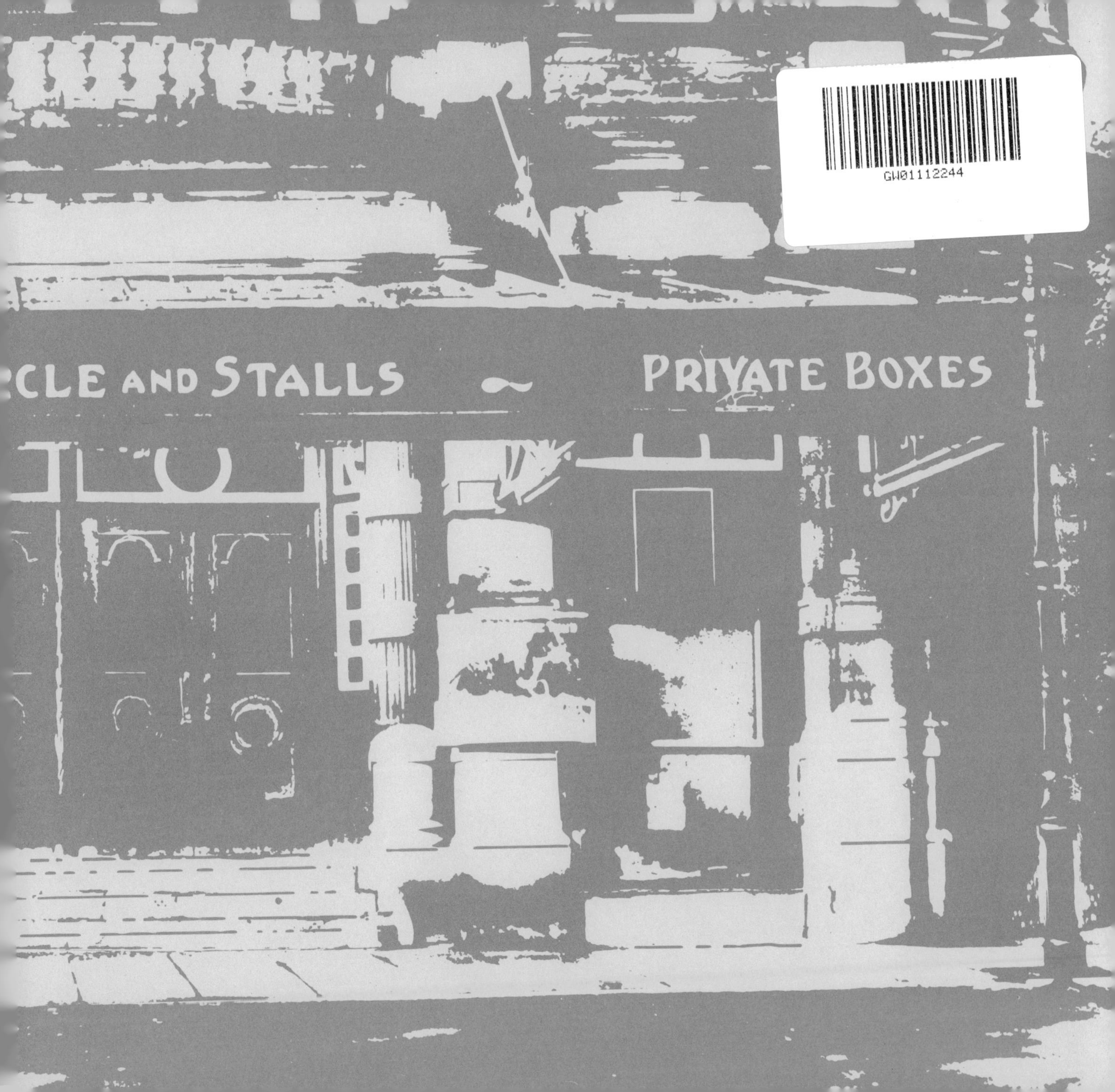
CLE AND STALLS
PRIVATE BOXES

THEATRE IN THE HILLS

TWO CENTURIES OF
THEATRE IN BUXTON

Copyright © Ros McCoola 1984

All rights reserved. No part of this publication may be reproduced or transmitted in any form or by any means without permission.

ISBN 0 947848 00 2

First published 1984
by Caron Publications
Peak Press Building
Eccles Road
Chapel-en-le-Frith
Derbyshire SK12 6HB

Typeset, designed and printed
in England by
PEAK PRESS LIMITED
Chapel-en-le-Frith
Derbyshire

Theatre in the Hills

TWO CENTURIES OF
THEATRE IN BUXTON

by

ROS McCOOLA

To the memory of my parents
Peter and Mary McCoola
1893-1977   1901-1982

*For John Scott
with all good wishes
Ros McCoola
September 1984*

caron
PUBLICATIONS

Chapel-en-le-Frith

His Grace The Duke of Devonshire PC MC
Patron: Buxton Opera House and Buxton Festival

FOREWORD

BY HIS GRACE THE DUKE OF DEVONSHIRE PC MC

I feel proud and privileged to write a brief foreword to this book on the theatre in Buxton. The town is very close to my heart and indeed one of my Christian names is Buxton. I had the honour to be its Mayor from 1952-54 and ever since I have had the good fortune to be closely involved in its multifarious activities.

The theatre has always been a strong element in the life of the town. This is not surprising considering the beauty of Matcham's Opera House recently so wonderfully restored. I remember as a boy being taken to see Lilian Baylis's productions in the late thirties while the recent opera festival was at once an outstanding success and goes from strength to strength. With the Opera House as its centre Buxton is becoming increasingly important as a centre of the arts in the north of England.

Acknowledgements

I thank His Grace the Duke of Devonshire for his kind foreword and for permission to work at Chatsworth. I am most grateful to His Grace, to the Trustees of the Chatsworth Settlement, to Mr Peter Day, Keeper of the Collections, to Mr Michael Pearman, Librarian, to Mr Hugo Read, CBE, former Agent and to Mrs Rosemary Marchant for most valuable help and material.

My debt is great to Dr Michael Bishop, Curator, and the staff of Buxton Art Gallery and Museum; to Mr Dickens, Editor, and staff of the Buxton *Advertiser;* to Mr Christopher Barron, Miss Jane Herbert and the staff of Buxton Opera House and Festival; to the Area Librarian and staff, Buxton Library; to Miss Joan Sinar, County Archivist, and staff of the Derbyshire Records Office; to Mr David Sorrell and staff of the County Museum Service and to staff of Caron Publications, Chapel-en-le-Frith; I thank them all sincerely.

I am grateful for the valuable help from Arup Associates, the Garrick Club, the Georgian Theatre at Richmond, Scarthin Books of Cromford, Bridge Street Bookshop of Buxton, the Society for Theatre Research and the staffs of libraries and museums where I have worked: Birmingham, Manchester, the British Museum, the Theatre Museum at the Victoria and Albert Museum and the Shakespeare Institute.

Space is limited; I can therefore merely name the following who have helped and encouraged me: Mr Jeff Clarke, Mrs Nellie Wain, Mrs Mildred Winterbotham, Mrs Norma Barclay, Mrs Jill Dick, Mr Geoffrey Ashton, Mrs Pat Tomlinson, Dr Hugh Torrens, Mr Shaun Sutton, Mr Charles Vance, Mr Joe Mitchenson, Miss Margery Willoughby, Mrs Cecily Williams, Miss Sybil Rosenfeld, Mr Iain Mackintosh, Mr Jack Reading, Mrs Anthony Hawtrey, Miss Jennifer Aylmer and the committee and members of the Willoughby Club.

I thank Dr Robert Hoult for the title, Mr Geoff Morgan for his photography and Mr Farquharson Cousins for typing the manuscript meticulously and helping with research.

Finally, and most particularly, I thank Mr Robert Mulholland, editor, printer and publisher, for his wonderful help and patience.

Photographic acknowledgements

For permission to include photographs and other illustrations the author is grateful to the following:- Arup Associates, Bovis, Buxton Advertiser, Buxton Arts Festival Ltd., Buxton Art Gallery and Museum, Martin Charles, Keith Clark, Mark Covell, Derbyshire Record Office, the Garrick Club, Georgian Theatre Richmond Trustees (photograph from a Bowers-Brittain original), Guy Gravett, Mrs A Hawtrey, High Peak Theatre Trust Ltd., Shuhei Iwamoto, the Mander and Mitchenson Collection, Methuen Ltd, Geoff Morgan, the Palace Hotel, Buxton, Shaun Sutton, Trustees of the Chatsworth Settlement, Margery Willoughby.

Every effort has been made to obtain permission to include the copyright material quoted or used in this book. The author apologises if any unwitting infringement has occurred.

Contents

Foreword by His Grace the Duke of Devonshire PC MC 5
Introduction 9
This Golden Half-Moon 11
A Mean Building 15
A Grand Place 29
The Entertainment Stage 39
A Real Gem 51
Festivals 73
A Joy for Generations to Come 91

List of Illustrations

His Grace the Duke of Devonshire PC MC 4
The Crescent, Buxton, 1797, *(Buxton Museum)* 8
Sites of the four Buxton theatres *(Richard Prime)* 9
Georgiana, First Countess Spencer *(Chatsworth)* 10
Georgiana, Fifth Duchess of Devonshire *(Chatsworth)* ..10
William, Fifth Duke of Devonshire *(Chatsworth)* 10
A View of Buxton, 1795 *(Buxton Museum)* 14
Playbill: *The Rivals*, 15 June 1790 *(Methuen Ltd)* 15
Robert William Elliston *(Garrick Club)* 16
Strollers in a Barn, William Hogarth *(Garrick Club)* 17
The Shakespeare Inn, Buxton, 1872 *(Buxton Museum)* ...18
William Spencer, Sixth Duke *(Chatsworth)* 19
Georgian Theatre, Richmond, Yorks *(Bowers-Brittain)* ..20
Application for Licence, 1788 *(Derbyshire Records)* 21
Playbill: *The Busybody*, 1792 *(Buxton Museum)* 22
Playbill: *The Dramatist* 1793 *(Buxton Museum)* 23
Playbill: *Soldier's Daughter* 1804 *(Buxton Museum)* 23
Thornill grave *(photograph: Geoff Morgan)* 24
Playbill: *As You Like It* 1804 *(Buxton Museum)* 24
John Kane's grave *(photograph: Geoff Morgan)* 24
Playbill: *The Broken Sword*, 1819 *(Buxton Museum)* 26
Edmund Kean as Richard III *(Mander & Mitchenson)* ...27
Hall Bank, Buxton *(Buxton Museum)* 28
Buxton Tithe Map, 1848 *(Derbyshire Record Office)*.....29
Extract: Chatsworth Accounts, 1854 *(Chatsworth)* 30
Arrears at Lady Day, 1851 *(Chatsworth)* 31
Playbill: *The Young Quaker*, 1834 *(Buxton Museum)* 32
View of Buxton *(Buxton Museum)* 33
Playbill: *School of Reform*, 1834 *(Buxton Museum)* 34
Playbill: *Rob Roy*, 1834 *(Buxton Museum)* 35
Playbill: *Poole the Outlaw*, 1837 *(Buxton Museum)* 37
The Duke's Bandstand *(Buxton Museum)* 38
William, Seventh Duke of Devonshire *(Chatsworth)* 39
Pavilion Gardens, Buxton *(Author's collection)* 41
Pavilion Theatre programme, 1891 *(Buxton Museum)* 42
Anthony Hawtrey *(Mrs Hawtrey's collection)* 43
J L Toole *(Buxton Museum)* 43
Hippodrome Cinema, Buxton *(Buxton Museum)* 45
Buxton Repertory Company: 1948 *(Shaun Sutton)* 46
Buxton Repertory Company Off Stage *(Shaun Sutton)* ...47
Gwen Watford and Allan Cuthbertson *(Shaun Sutton)* ...47
Patrick Cargill and Julie Mortimer *(Shaun Sutton)* 47
Frank Matcham *(Buxton Museum)* 48
Arthur Willoughby *(Buxton Museum)* 48
Colour: 1903 Programme Cover 49
1903 Programme, inside page *(Buxton Museum)* 50
Colour: Opera House *(Mark Covell)* 52
John Willoughby *(Miss M Willoughby)* 54
Colour: Opera House stage *(Arup Associates)* 53
Colour: Opera House auditorium *(Arup Associates)* 56
Colour: Matcham plan *(Arup Associates)* 57
Colour: Interior Opera House *(Arup Associates)* 60
Programme cover 1907 *(Buxton Museum)* 61
Playbill: *Mrs Willoughby's Kiss*, 1903 *(Buxton Museum)* ..63
Programme 1903 *(Buxton Museum)* 63
Douglas Fairbanks & Mary Pickford *(Palace Hotel)* 68
Anna Pavlova *(Buxton Museum)* 69
Opera House staff, 1932 *(Advertiser)* 71
Old Vic Festival programme, 1937 *(Buxton Museum)* 73
Postcard from George Bernard Shaw *(Buxton Museum)* ..74
Lilian Baylis *(Buxton Museum)* 75
Plaque: Buxton Opera House *(Geoff Morgan)* 77
Robert Morley and Diana Wynyard *(Buxton Museum)* ...79
Alec Guinness *(Buxton Museum)* 80
Strand Electric Grand Master *(Arup Associates)* 81
Sunlight Gas Panel *(Arup Associates)* 81
Robert Donat, Constance Cummings, *(Buxton Museum)* ..83
Water ingress, Upper circle *(Advertiser)* 85
Among the scaffolding, 1979 *(Bovis)* 86
Royal Visit, 1978 *(Advertiser)* 86
Sir John Betjeman *(Keith Clark)* 87
Deborah Cook *(Christopher Reece-Bowan)* 88
Lucia di Lammermoor *(Guy Gravett)* 89
Malcolm Fraser, Artistic Director, Buxton Festival 90
Anthony Hose, Musical Director, Buxton Festival 90
Monica Pick-Hieronimi *(Guy Gravett)* 90
Sir Spencer Le Marchant *(Shuhei Iwamoto)* 93
David Hunter, Chairman, Buxton Festival 93
Christopher Barron, General Manager 93
Thomas Allen, Christine Barbaux *(Guy Gravett)* 94
Rosalind Plowright *(Fritz Curzon)* 95
Sir Geraint Evans *(Shuhei Iwamoto)* 95
Philip Langridge & Ann Murray *(Guy Gravett)* 95
Cast of James and the Giant Peach *(Shuhei Iwamoto)* ...95

The Crescent, Buxton.
Aquatint by William Martin F L S 1767-1810, distinguished geologist and artist who performed in the Buxton theatre in the 1790s.

Introduction

A remote village in the hills of the High Peak is an unlikely place to have any kind of theatre history. Buxton might have remained a simple Derbyshire village to this day, its inhabitants content to make their own homespun amusements, had not the Fifth Duke of Devonshire, aware of the appeal and usefulness of its thermal and chalybeate springs, decided to develop it as a spa. There is no evidence that the Duke intended to provide a theatre among the splendid buildings which John Carr of York designed for him, but almost as soon as the Crescent, Carr's masterpiece, was completed in 1784, the town's theatre history began.

It is an uncomplicated history, and something of a rags-to-riches story. Climate, geographical position and near-impossible roads much of the year, dictated a short bathing and theatre season in eighteenth and early nineteenth century Buxton. After the arrival of the first railway in 1863, the town expanded rapidly, and theatre seasons extended until eventually the Opera House was open for fifty weeks in the year.

Buxton has had four theatres in the last two hundred years, all situated in the lower part of the town where visitors most congregate. The first was a small, mean, thatched building in Spring Gardens; the second, still small, but more impressive, at least to Buxtonians, stood where Broad Walk and Hartington Road now meet opposite the Old Hall Hotel. The third, the "maid-of-all-work" of Buxton theatres (the Playhouse), formed part of the Pavilion complex of buildings, opening on to St. John's Road; the fourth, still standing, is the Opera House, Frank Matcham's masterpiece, and now the theatre for the whole High Peak community. The town may have had two or three other theatres in the early period, but apart from a single reference to each in a guide book or newspaper, no evidence of their existence is so far forthcoming, and so they are not discussed here.

The generosity of successive Dukes of Devonshire is reflected in the history of the four theatres described, as it is in the history of most Buxton institutions. In the account which follows, contemporary descriptions, records and reminiscences have been quoted somewhat extensively. They make more vivid reading than paraphrases and third-hand accounts can produce. The book is very much a work-in-progress; there is still much to discover, much more to tell. A theatre archive has been established at Buxton Museum. If this book encourages Buxtonians to deposit there the fascinating theatre ephemera which lie forgotten in attics, cupboards and drawers, it will have served a useful purpose.

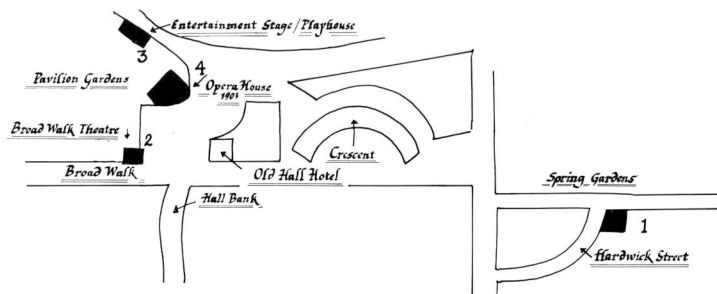

Diagram not to scale, showing positions of the four theatres discussed in this book: (1) Spring Gardens 1784(?)-1829(?). (2) Broad Walk 1830(?)-1854. (3) Pavilion Gardens 1889-1979 but now the Paxton Suite. (4) The Opera House 1903-.

Top left: *Georgiana, First Countess Spencer 1737-1814.*
Lower left: *Georgiana, Fifth Duchess of Devonshire 1757-1806.*
Above: *William, Fifth Duke of Devonshire 1748-1811.*

CHAPTER ONE

This Golden Half Moon

WRITING from Buxton on Saturday 10 May 1783 to her daughter Georgiana, Fifth Duchess of Devonshire, the first Countess Spencer, an ancestor of our much loved Princess of Wales, complains of an uncomfortable journey and diabolical weather,[1]

> the place here some 50 degrees more dreary and dismal than my memory had represented it.

She asks her daughter to thank the Duke[2] for supplies sent from Chatsworth

> without which I know not what we should have done ....not a cabbage an onion or a bunch of Parsley is to be got at this place...

but at last she sounds a hopeful note with her reference to the Crescent, now nearing completion:

> The Duke's Buildings here are very magnificent indeed and the plantations on the tops of the surrounding hills which are begun and I am told are to be continued are a glorious work and will in time be as beneficial as beautiful.

In September of the same year, the Duchess herself visited Buxton. In a letter to her mother she declares:[3]

> I never saw anything so magnificent as the Crescent - though it must half ruin one, my spirit makes me delight in the Duke's doing it.

A year later, the magnificent edifice was completed. So too, in due course, were the Great Stables, the first five houses of Hall Bank, the Square and St John's Church. Tree planting continued and the stage was set for the development of a fashionable spa in Derbyshire, to rival the flourishing Bath spa in Somerset. Sixty years earlier, Daniel Defoe had seen Buxton's potential. In his *Tour Through the Whole Island of Great Britain* (1724-26), he describes his journey over the "howling wilderness" towards Buxton, with "a most frightful view indeed among the black mountains of the Peak". He is somewhat scornful of most of the so-called Wonders of the Peak, but praises Buxton waters, and suggests that if

> the nobility and gentry were suitably entertained, I doubt not but Buxton would be frequented, and with more effect as to health, as well as much more satisfaction to the company; where there is an open and healthy country, a great variety of view to satisfy the curious, and fine down or moor for the ladies to take a ring upon their coaches, all much more convenient than in a close city as Bath is.....

Thanks to the Fifth Duke's buildings, Buxton now had elegant accommodation for fashionable visitors. The Crescent provided hotels, lodgings and shops; Hall Bank offered quiet boarding houses.

Anna Seward,[4] daughter of a vicar of Eyam who later became a Canon of Lichfield Cathedral, was a frequent visitor to the town. Her stilted prose records the scene about this "golden half-moon", the Crescent, in a letter to her friend Miss Ponsonby in 1796, and shows that within a dozen years, the town was certainly "frequented":

> Buxton is growing very full, not withstanding this unnatural weather. I now sit writing by a good fire, in very commodious lodgings. My neat little parlour looks backward, is on the first flight of stairs, and, from its aspect, is quiet and silent. When I close one of the sash windows, that looks on the superb stables, which are built on the rise of the hill, above this splendid, this golden half-moon, the other window

---

[1] From unpublished correspondence at Chatsworth.
[2] The Fifth Duke, William (1748-1811).
[3] Chatsworth correspondence.
[4] Anna Seward. Letters: 1784-1807. Published in six volumes. George Ramsey, Edinburgh, 1811.

shows me only a sloping range of bare fields, without hedge or tree, and intersected by stone walls. They present a perfect picture of a barren country, of rudeness, silence and solitude. I am gratified by meditating the striking contrast, when, quitting this apartment, half a minute conveys me into the "busiest hum of men"; amid a crowd of old and young, grave and gay, feeble and frolicsome, blighted and blooming, that sweep, in long trains, through the arcade; while in the area of its concave, horses and horsemen are prancing, and chariots and phaetons swiftly roll.

Colonel Byng,[5] writing six years earlier, points out a few disadvantages:

> The sick and lame, who come to bathing places shou'd live in lower floors, in private lodgings, and shou'd not be hoisted up in great noisy hotels. - The Duke of D[evonshire] being seized upon by some builder, has here lavished his money upon an huge mausoleum! And this, like his copper-mine, may one day, be exhausted; for these waters depend upon fashion, and the whim of the physicians. - The piazzas are too narrow to defend from either sun, or rain; and the shops exhibit no temptation, like those of Tunbridge.

Colonel Byng admired "the great and fine assembly room, card rooms and dining room" (even whilst scorning John Carr of York's handsome Crescent, built for the Duke of Devonshire and paid for from the profits of the Duke's Ecton copper mine.) Old guide books list these and other, mainly out-door, attractions. Several mention the theatre. Perhaps the most informative and interesting account of what Buxton offered for the entertainment of visitors occurs in Jewitt's[6] *History of Buxton* (1811). He quotes a letter, written from Hall Bank in August 1810, in which an "amiable young lady" conveys "a good idea of the manner in which visitors of taste in general pass their time". She recounts "a round of ever-varying amusement."

On Sunday, after rising at 6 to drink the waters and to walk round Anne's Cliffe, she and her brother went to bathe with their aunt and uncle, the women to the ladies' private bath, the men to theirs. At 11, after breakfast, they heard divine service in the Assembly Room:

> Perhaps before the expiration of another season the church[7] which his Grace of Devonshire is building may be completed. It is a fine building, and will be worthy to rank with the Crescent.

At dinner they signed the subscription book for the Charitable Institution,[8] thus binding themselves to donate a shilling (not enough! thought the young lady) for the fund for poor people "recommended to the waters", and in the evening took a turn along the new walks.[9] At six on Monday morning, the party set out for Castleton, arriving about ten, and returned via Bradwell and Tideswell. They went to the Assembly at 8 in the evening, "better attended by ladies than gentlemen," since all the young male visitors had been out grouse shooting all day (August 12th) and were too tired to "engage in a dance" at their return. Tuesday morning was devoted to a visit to Poole's Hole and a ramble among the lime houses.[10] Rain in the afternoon reduced them to an hour's walking in the arcade, "a very convenient promenade for bad weather", and a visit to Mr Moore's library in the Crescent to which they subscribed, then the ladies returned to read while the gentlemen adjourned to the Billiard Room.[11] After tea they all went to the theatre.

---

[5] The Torrington Diaries, containing the Tours through England and Wales of the Honourable John Byng, later Viscount Torrington, between the years 1781 and 1794. 4 volumes. Edited by C. Bruyn Andrews. Barnes & Noble Inc. New York. Methuen & Co Ltd, London.

[6] The History of Buxton and Visitor's Guide to the History of the Peak. A. Jewitt. Published by the Author. 2nd edition 1816.

[7] St John's Church opened August 1812.

[8] Visitors were asked to subscribe one shilling to the Bath Charity to enable poor people to take the waters.

[9] Presumably the walks about the Crescent and the Slopes.

[10] Jewitt describes them: "habitations ... with which the sides of the hills contiguous to the lime kilns are almost universally covered." He condemns them as "wretched and disgusting" caves, and includes an illustration p107 (2nd edition) of one of these crude dwellings.

[11] Jewitt: Billiard Tables - Of these Buxton has three.

Since Wednesday morning was "unfavourable", the young lady employed herself with Garnett's *Tour into Scotland,* the book she had borrowed from Mr Moore's Library. The party walked to Lover's Leap in the afternoon, and the young lady indulged her passion for botanising, in the dell and among the rocks. They went to the dress-ball in the evening, the Assembly room appearing "uncommonly brilliant", thanks to an influx of arrivals "of the first fashion" that day. On Thursday morning they made a family party to a concert, took an airing on horseback in the afternoon and attended the Theatre once more in the evening. Friday morning was devoted to a visit to Chee Torr and Miller's Dale. In the afternoon, "the weather continuing extremely fine", they walked to the top of Ax-edge, which rendered them incapable of attending the Assembly in the evening. A good night's rest restored them, and at six on Saturday morning, in three chaises, they set out for Chatsworth. They admired the house and countryside, but found the water-works inferior. Returning to Buxton around 6 pm, having visited Hassop, Great Longstone and Monsal Dale, they concluded their first week in Buxton with another visit to the Theatre. Ever varying amusement indeed!

To provide it, Buxton had made gratifying progress in less than thirty years since the completion of the Crescent in 1784. Visiting the town in that year, Monsieur B. Faujas de Saint Fond,[12] a geologist, found the seven hour journey from Manchester "neither agreeable nor commodious". Excellent though its waters were, he considered the air "impregnated with sorrow and melancholy" and disliked the houses, "like hospitals or rather monkish buildings". He did, however, admire the Crescent:

> An imposing fine erection in a grand and beautiful style of architecture, which is seen at the bottom of the place, and is appropriated to the baths, might be taken for the palace of an abbot.

In addition to the space occupied by the baths, he informs us, the Crescent offered accommodation for two hundred guests, exclusively of room for their servants, for the attendants at the baths and wells, and for the various innkeepers and caterers, these last the principal tenants of the entire structure:

> The whole of this fabric, erected at the expense of the Duke of Devonshire, after the plans and under the superintendence of the architect Carr,[13] is in a good style of architecture, uniting to an air of grandeur a feeling of taste, which does honour to the talents of that able artist, whom I had the pleasure of seeing, and who was kind enough to conduct me through every part of it.

From such testimony, contrasting it with the information we glean from Jewitt's "amiable young lady", from Anna Seward and others, we realise what an enormous debt Buxton owes to the Fifth Duke of Devonshire and his successors for their long-sustained benevolence. Let us now discover what theatrical entertainment the town provided as the years rolled by.

---

12   B. Faujas de Saint Fond: A Journey through Scotland and England in 1784. Edited by A. Geikie, 1907.

13   John Carr of York (1723-1807).

A View of Buxton from Fairfield Hill
Aquatint by William Martin F L S 1795

The large dark building almost obliterating the Crescent is the Grove Inn. Was the theatre the small building immediately in front of the Grove? It is similar to a drawing of Sadlers Wells in an unpublished part of James Winston's The Theatric Tourist, a valuable source of information about 18th Century provincial theatres.

CHAPTER TWO
A Mean Building

WE gather from the young lady writing from Hall Bank in 1810 that she and her party went to the Theatre on Tuesday, Thursday and Saturday evenings:

> What a mean building! but for the words Pit and Boxes over the door, it would be mistaken for a barn. We found it much prettier within; it was newly painted, and the performers were better than we could have expected on such a stage; some indeed were excellent in their line.

A coat or two of paint in 1810 appears to have wrought miracles; twenty years earlier, in 1790, Colonel Byng was much less kind and enthusiastic. Staying at the Old Angel, Macclesfield, he notes:

> I shall be sorry not to see some players, as I hear of them around, as at Leek, and at Manchester; and that they will soon be at Buxton....

He reached Buxton in June, but did not stay to see a play. He admits that during a morning walk he went in to look at the Theatre. His verdict:

> a mean, dirty, boarded, thatched house; and can hold but few people.

Poor Colonel Byng! he did not like Buxton. Most of his comments have grudging undertones. How useful of him, even so, to include the playbill[1] for the first performance of the season at the Theatre and the card for the Ball at the Assembly Room!

That the Buxton Theatre (and company) left much to be desired before that refurbishing in 1810 is demonstrated by George Raymond,[2] in *Memoirs of Robert William Elliston*, comedian. He covers Elliston's career between

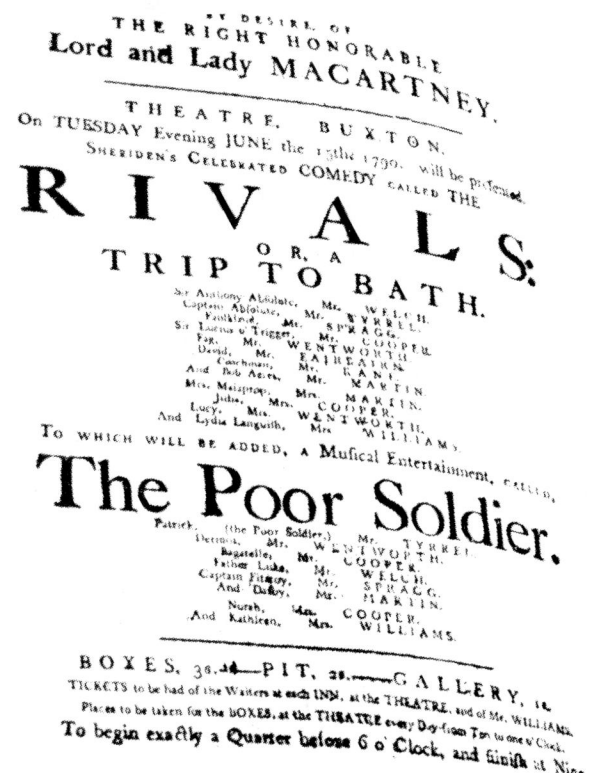

Playbill for Sheridan's The Rivals at Buxton June 15 1790.

1774 and 1810. In 1807, after a flattering reception in Liverpool, Elliston decided upon a leisurely return to London. One detour brought him to Buxton, where he acted for three or four nights. Admitting that country theatricals are ready objects of ridicule, Raymond nevertheless proceeds to cast a mocking, sophisticated eye upon the Buxton brand. The Theatre, he pronounces, is "miserable". It has only two scenes

> which, like Master Solomon's waistcoat, had been turned for many occasions, and from their state of

---

1. For a performance of Sheridan's *The Rivals* on Tuesday June 15, 1790.
2. Memoirs of Robert William Elliston, comedian, 1774 to 1810 by George Raymond Esq., with illustrations by George Cruickshank. Published John Mortimer, London, 1844.

near obliteration had arrived at such a point of utility as to pass for anything... A few stage "foot-lamps" illumed the whole house, throwing a dim irreligious light upon the fresco brick wall, which supported both the roof of the building and the back of the spectator.

The pit floor was composed of a line of hurdles because, apparently, the low position of the Theatre rendered it liable to flooding "in the rainy season".

The scant wardrobe, to the last thread and button, was, it is true, employed in every piece, but which, being a contribution of all costumes under the sun, was at least, in some character, (like the child's sham watch), right once during the evening.

The company was small in number, but

> with the exception of two urchins, who had but one hat between them, there was not an actor or actress much under seventy years of age.

On Elliston's first night in Buxton, the entertainment was *The Castle Spectre,* in the course of which one unfortunate actor, doubling parts, had to play both parts on stage at the same time, carrying on the dialogue with himself. His difficulties did not end there; at two points in the dialogue he had to put head and shoulders through a small aperture, to have a fiddle handed to him by someone back stage so that he could himself supply the off stage music twice referred to in his dialogue with himself! The first attempt was successful.

> Once again, head and shoulders through the window, the fiddle raised to his hands, on he went -
> "To spring below then never dread,
> Our arms to catch you shall be spread;
> A boat now waits to set you free..."

But alas! just at this moment, when in act of a second time pulling in his body from the narrow aperture, the exertion necessary to the operation, together with the fragile state of the antique scenery, produced a most awful crash - the whole side of Osmond's castle wall, with Muley sticking in the window-frame, like a rat caught by his neck, fell inwards on the stage, disclosing at one view an heterogeneous state of

Robert William Elliston (1774-1831) actor and theatre manager who in 1819 achieved his ambition of managing Drury Lane. A fascinating, extravagant man, he was praised and admired by Leigh Hunt, Charles Lamb and other contemporary critics.

things beyond, beggaring all powers of description. Hogarth's *Strollers Dressing in a Barn* is not more fantastically conceived...

Hogarth's Strollers Dressing in a Barn depicts the difficult conditions endured by itinerant actors in the provinces in 18th Century England.

The Shakespeare Inn, Spring Gardens, Buxton. The inn endured, much altered, until 1926, when the Woolworth emporium took over part of the site.

Each night brought disaster. On the second night, when Elliston's favourite, *Aranza,* was presented, all was going well before a packed house:

> Juliana (in the costume of Fatima!) was, it is true, as imperfect in her part as person; yet had she retained the very words of her author, she would scarcely have been more distinct, for she had lost every tooth in her head...

Disaster came in Act Four. Jaques, rising from his chair, caught his sword in the old curtain thrown over the chair to give it a more luxurious appearance, only to reveal that the "chair", borrowed for the occasion from the neighbouring Inn, was in fact a commode, "originally fashioned for the incidental purposes of a sick chamber."

The people absolutely screamed with merriment - in fact, they laughed for a whole week afterwards.

Fortunately matters improved; the Reverend D. P. Davies (1811)[3] assures us that

> a small commodious theatre is usually well filled by a genteel audience three evenings a week

---

[3] Reverend D. P. Davies: A New Historical and Descriptive View of Derbyshire, 1811.

William Spencer, Sixth Duke of Devonshire 1790-1858.

and even better, Henry Moore (1820)[4] declares

> The Theatre is a very mean looking building but the interior is neatly fitted up; and the company of performers very respectable; so that the kernel proves good, although the shell is unpromising.

Where was this mean building, so regularly filled by a genteel audience? Jewitt (1811) does not give its location, but tells us that it was built at or about the same time as the Great Stables. He claims that it was erected by the manager of the company

> which previously to that time performed in a barn which stood on part of the ground now occupied by these Stables.

Until more precise information is forthcoming, it seems reasonable to accept the statement of a Victorian Buxtonian that this Theatre stood in or near what is now Spring Gardens, on the site occupied (until the early 1960s) by Messrs J. Milligan and Sons, drapery establishment, and now occupied by International Stores. No doubt the Shakespeare Inn built nearby was so named in compliment to the Theatre. Jewitt concedes that the Theatre exterior was "mean in the extreme", but it is reassuring to know that

> within it is well fitted up and maybe pronounced a pretty little theatre....
> As it is only open during the bathing season, and as at that time the London theatres are in general closed, the best actors from these boards are generally engaged here in succession, which, with a regular company far above mediocrity, affords a rational entertainment to those visitors whose maladies will permit them to enjoy this amusement.

The lease had almost expired in 1811:

> ....in consequence, it is to be hoped that His Grace, who has already done so much for Buxton, will build another more agreeable to the improved state of the place, and more comfortable for the audience. (Jewitt)

Alas! almost as Jewitt was going to press, the Fifth Duke died in August 1811,

> in much the manner he had lived - quietly, dropsically and very late at night.[5]

He was succeeded by his son, a charming young man of twenty one, who, although never noticeably averse to building, and undoubtedly a great benefactor to Buxton, had many matters pressing for attention when he came into his inheritance; a handsome theatre for Buxton was not one of them.

---

[4] Henry Moore: Picturesque Excursions in the High Peak of Derbyshire, 1820.
[5] John Pearson: *Stags and Serpents*. The story of the House of Cavendish and the Dukes of Devonshire, p116. Published Macmillan, 1983.

The Georgian Theatre, Richmond, Yorkshire.

No picture of the "Spring Gardens" Theatre has come down to us. It is tempting to think that one of the barnlike structures on the left of William Martin's aquatint, *A View of Buxton from Fairfield Hill,*[6] dated 1796, was the theatre in which he and his mother played in the 1790s, and to which he returned annually for a few years after he left Buxton, to give performances and to take a benefit. Martin was a compulsive illustrator and recorder. Surely the scene of his nightly toil would not be omitted?

Those familiar with the Georgian Theatre at Richmond in Yorkshire, built by Samuel Butler in 1788 and lovingly restored in 1963, will have some idea of the external and internal appearance of the theatre of the same period in Buxton. Externally, the Richmond theatre is not unlike the stone barns we see in the Yorkshire and Derbyshire Dales. It is a tall building, 28ft. by 81ft., and almost without windows. Internally, it is intimate and welcoming. To twentieth century eyes it seems incredibly small. The proscenium is only 18 feet wide and 20 feet high. The auditorium has boxes at stage level, four down each of the two sides and three on the back wall facing the stage. A dramatist's name appears over each box. The name over the centre box (the Royal box) is in the original lettering: Shakespeare. How fitting that that name should endure! Below stage level is the Pit, 18 feet square, with bench seats, reached via passage ways under the side boxes. Above the three centre boxes is the Gallery, rectangular, with bench seats. These were "knife-edge"

---

[6] This aquatint may be seen at Buxton Art Gallery and Museum.

To his Majesty's Justices of the Peace for the County of Derby at the general Quarter Sessions assembled at Bakewell in and for the said County on Tuesday the twenty ninth day of July 1788 —

The humble petition of John Welch and John Ferrizer on behalf of themselves and their Company of Comedians now being at Buxton within the said County —

Your Petitioners in pursuance of an Act passed in the last Session of Parliament Intituled "An Act to enable Justices of the Peace to licence Theatrical Representations occasionally under the Restrictions therein contained" Do humbly petition this Court, to grant them a licence as prescribed by the said Act, for the performance of such Plays and Interludes as are mentioned therein at Bakewell within this County from the first day of October to the Nineteenth day of November next —

July 30. 1788.

And your Petitioners shall ever pray &c

John Welch
John Ferrizer

Application made from Buxton by John Welch and John Ferrizer to present plays at Bakewell 30 July 1788.

benches - no soft upholstery for Georgian galleryites! And close-packed audiences were obviously the rule; the theatre seated over 400 in the 1780s; it now seats 238. To watch a play in such an auditorium is enchanting. It can prove almost overwhelming if the play is powerful; actors and audience are in close proximity, and everyone can see and be seen without difficulty.

Richmond was once part of a theatre circuit which included Northallerton, Ripon, Harrogate, Beverley, Kendal, Ulverston and Whitby. The Theatre is now open daily, 2.30 to 5.30, May to September, so that visitors may see it, but no theatre lover should miss the experience of seeing an evening performance there.

John Welch was manager of the Buxton company in 1788, the year he and John Ferrizer applied for a licence "on behalf of themselves and their company of comedians" to perform "Plays and Interludes" at Bakewell "from the first day of October to the 19th day of November next" (dated 30 July 1788). An Act had been passed empowering JPs to license "Theatrical Representations" within stated limits, and it is interesting to see Welch and his company taking advantage of this, no doubt hoping to make money in a neighbouring town when the Buxton theatre season closed.

A Prologue reminds us of the hard, uncertain life which has usually been the lot of the majority of actors:

> Hard is the Fortune of a strolling Play'r!
> Necessity's rough Burden doom'd to bear:
> And scanty is the Pittance he can earn,
> Wand'ring from Town to Town, from Barn to Barn.
> This might content us but the Contrast great
> Adds to the Terror of our changeful Fate.
> He who to Night is seated on his Throne
> Calls Subjects, Kingdoms, Empires, all his own.
> Who wears the Diadem and Regal Robe
> Next morning shall awake - As poor as Job.
> 'Where are my forty Knights?' cries frantic Lear.
> A Page replies - 'Your Majesty, they're here!
> When lo! Two Bailiffs and a Writ appear.
> 'Give me a Pound of Flesh', cries Shylock, well he may,
> For Shylock - has not eat an Ounce to Day.

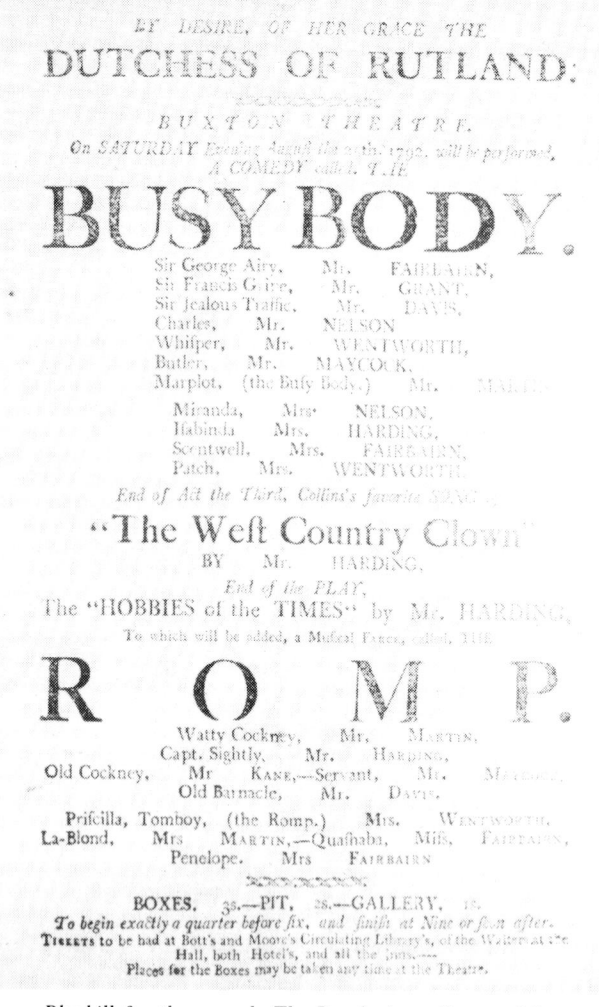

Playbill for the comedy The Busybody at Buxton, 25 August 1792.

Welch, like succeeding managers had a stock company, and some members were obviously capable actors. When a London actor was engaged for the Buxton season, members of the company would have to be ready to support him in whatever plays he chose. Prodigious feats

Playbill 1

By Desire of the MOST NOBLE THE
MARQUIS OF DROGHEDA.

For the Benefit of Mrs Williams.

On SATURDAY Evening September the 7 1793 will be perform'd,
A COMEDY, (not acted this Season,) call'd THE

DRAMATIST
Or, Stop him who Can.

Vapid, (the Dramatist) Mr. WILLIAMS,
Ennui, Mr. MARTIN,
Lord Scratch, Mr. CRANESON,
Neville Mr. GRANT,
Willoughby, Mr. WENTWORTH,
Peter, Mr KANE.—Servant Mr. BAILEY,
Florival, Mr. FAIRBAIRN,
Mariana, Mrs. WILLIAMS
Lady Waitfort Mrs. MARTIN,
Letty, Mrs. FAIRBAIRN,
Louisa Mrs. WENTWORTH.

End of the PLAY COLLINS's NEW SONG, called THE
CHAPTER OF KINGS" by Mr WILLIAMS.
To which will be added, reduced to an After piece THE

Highland Reel.

Mc'Gilpin Mr WELCH—Charley Mr MARTIN
Sandy Mr WENTWORTH—Serjt. Jack Mr CRANESON,
Capt Dash Mr. FAIRBAIRN—Bairn Master FAIRBAIRN,
Laird Donald, Mr. KANE—Laird of Racey Mr. BROWN
Shelty. Mr WILLIAMS.
Moggy, Mrs WILLIAMS.
Jenny Mrs WENTWORTH
Ladies the rest of the LADIES.

To conclude with a REEL by the CHARACTERS.

Boxes, 3s—Pit, 2s—Gal 1s
To begin exactly at 6 o'Clock—Places may be taken at the Theatre,
Tickets to be had at the Wells at Bath and M's Library s and
of Mrs. WILLIAMS at Mr. Gregory's.

Playbill 2

THEATRE BUXTON.

FOR THE BENEFIT OF
MRS. SAVILLE,

On Thursday Aug. 23d 1805 will be presented the COMEDY of
THE
Soldier's Daughter.

Governor Heartall   Mr. BENGOUGH
Frank Heartall   Mr. GORDON
Malfort Senior   Mr. CUMBERLAND
Malfort Junior   Mr. JONES
Cap. Woolley   Mr. MILLS
Mr. Ferret   Mr. ANDERSON
Timothy Quaint   Mr. PENSON
Simon   Mr. MARTIN
Tom Mr. JOHNSON   Footman Mr. MAYCOCK

The Widow Cheerly (with the Original Epilogue)   Mrs. SAVILLE
Mrs. Malfort   Miss JONES
Julia   Miss HATTON
Susan   Mrs. BENGOUGH
Mrs. Fidget   Mrs. READ

END OF THE PLAY
A Comic Song
CALLED "THE DRILL'D RECRUIT"
BY MR. PENSON

To which will be added The FARCE of
The Citizen,

Old Philpot Mr. PENSON   Young Philpot Mr. MILLS
Sir Jasper Wilding   Mr. CUMBERLAND
Young Wilding   Mr. BENGOUGH
Beaufort Mr. JONES   Quilldrive Mr. JOHNSON
Maria   Mrs SAVILLE
Corinna   Mrs. BENGOUGH

Boxes 4s. Pit 2s. 6d. Gall. 1s. 6d.
Second Price to Gall. [End of 2 Act] 1s.
Tickets to be had, and Places for the Boxes to be taken. from
9. till 3 o'clock at Mr. Moore's Library, Crescent, and of Mrs. Saville
at Mr. Clayton's Shoe-Maker below the Theatre.
Doors to be opened at 5, and to begin precisely at 6 o'clock
Cope, Printer.

Two Buxton playbills: The Dramatist and The Soldier's Daughter. Note the second price for entry after the end of the second act.

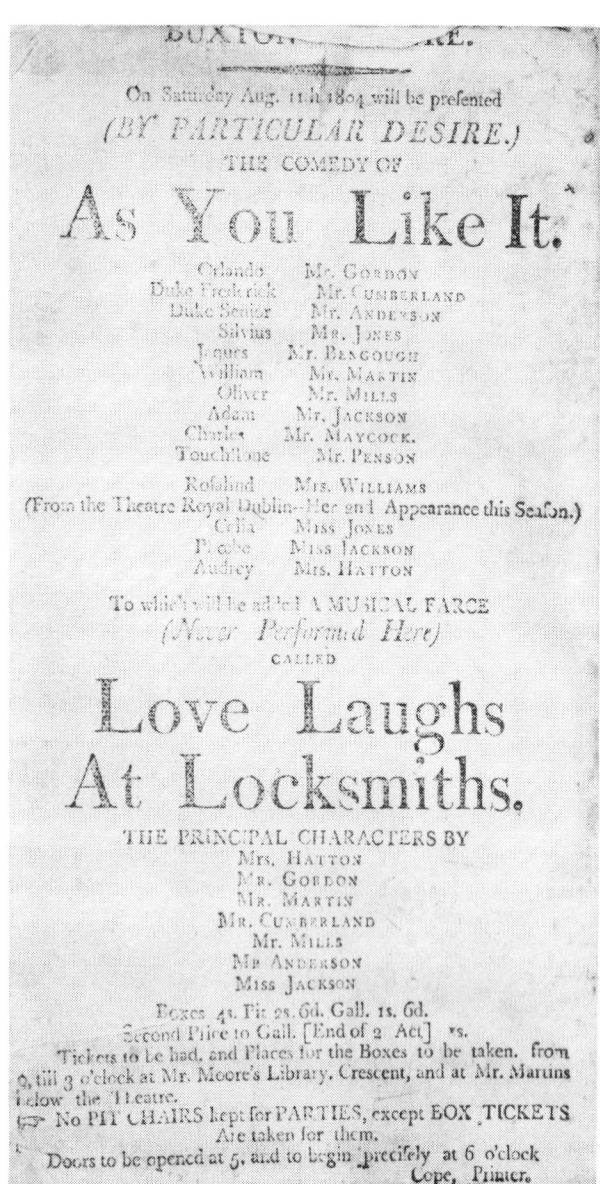

Playbill for Shakespeare's As You Like It at Buxton Theatre 1804.

Grave (above) of members of a famous theatrical family in Buxton, the Thornhills (spelled Thornill on the grave.) Below: Grave of John Kane, actor in the Buxton company in the 1790s. Both graves may still be seen in St Anne's churchyard, Buxton.

of memory would be necessary, and the prompter would have to be alert!

S. W. Ryley (he acted under the name S. W. Romney)[7] was connected with the Buxton company for many years, possibly from as early as 1787. He wrote a kind of autobiography, *The Itinerant,* in nine volumes, but since he rarely includes dates, his writings are not always the precise source of information we should like them to be. If only he had emulated Colonel Byng and included theatre bills among his anecdotes! The 1790 Buxton playbill quoted by the Colonel tells us that Sheridan's *The Rivals* was presented "By desire of the Right Honourable Lord and Lady Macartney". Provincial theatre managers were always delighted to give performances "by desire" of some notable person, expecting that person to bring a crowd of friends with him and to recompense the manager handsomely.

The Buxton company in 1790 consisted of Messrs Welch, Tyrrel, Spragg, Cooper, Wentworth, Fairbairn, Kane, Martin and Williams; the women, obviously related to the male actors, were Mrs Martin, Mrs Cooper, Mrs Wentworth, Mrs Williams, Mrs Welch, Mrs Fairbairn and Miss Butler. Two of these names still have significance for us today: Martin and Kane. William Martin (1767-1810), said to have been particularly good in foppish parts, was a distinguished geologist, and no mean artist, if we are to judge by the two examples of his work extant in Buxton Art Gallery and Museum. He published *Figures and Descriptions of Petrifactions Collected in Derbyshire* in 1793, and wrote other books and papers on fossils. He was much respected as a geologist, not least for his coherent classification of fossils and his detailed drawings of them. He was honoured as a Fellow of the Linnaean Society. His life cannot have been easy. It is hardly surprising that he died at a comparatively early age, leaving a wife and children, alas! not well provided for. His mother, the Mrs Martin on the playbills, was an experienced actress, compelled to return to the stage when she and her son were callously abandoned by her husband. William Martin left Buxton in 1805 and lived in Macclesfield where he taught art at the Grammar School. He was not a born actor but obviously reliable and hard working. He did achieve one outstanding success: in the farce *The Farmer*. He was so entertaining as Jemmy Jumps that the play ran to packed houses for ten nights. Tate Wilkinson[8] was so impressed that he offered him a place in his company at York, but Martin declined. Too far from his fossils, no doubt!

Kane, the second name still significant, is that of John Kane (1741-99), an actor who came from Dublin, already middle aged when he joined the Buxton company. He was a likeable man, apparently, but sadly fond of alcohol. There is more than a suggestion that his charming personality and easy temperament, rather than his prowess on stage, assured him a place in the company. He died on 10 November 1799 as a result of eating hemlock with his beef. He had gathered it himself, thinking it to be horse radish. He was buried in St Anne's churchyard. His grave may be seen there, facing west, whilst others near, all face east. When this was pointed out to the famous Victorian comedian, J. L. Toole, who visited the grave in 1889, he was pensive for a moment, then, indicating the other graves with an expansive gesture, declared with a smile "Think of the audience he will have on Judgment Day!" Toole paid for the grave to be refurbished. It has again fallen into some disrepair. Will a twentieth century comedian save it this time? Another gravestone of considerable interest lies cracked in two on the ground near Kane's. It records several members of the Thornhill family, most of whom were connected with theatre in Buxton. George Thornhill was here from 1782. He died on 24 December 1801 aged 52. Perhaps it was his brother of whom Ryley writes around 1809:

> I made no further halt until we reached Buxton. I had always entertained a strong partiality for this place. The air - the bathing - were to me so invigorating and attended with such beneficial effects in point of health, that I never approached it without pleasure, or left it without regret. The theatre was under the management of Mr Thornhill, an indefatigable labourer in the histrionic art, who had for years been attempting to roll the dramatic millstone up the hill

---

[7] S. W. Ryley: The Itinerant in 9 volumes. 1817.

[8] Tate Wilkinson *The Wandering Patentee*. 1795.

of success; but like Sisyphus, he found every effort produced a retrograde motion; still he persevered, animated by the hope of ultimately providing for a wife and ten children! He had long steered his theatrical bark amidst the shoals and quicksands of Lancashire, and though seldom favoured with a prosperous gale, still contrived - because backed by honesty and good intentions - to keep above water. Buxton was his sheet anchor, and I found both the manager and his company spoken well of by the visitors. The morning after my arrival, I made it my business to call upon Manager Thornhill, who was a plain downright kind of fellow, who thought himself no better than the members of his company, and could exist without toothpicks and bang-up coats, shining boots and tweezers.

During Thornhill's time as manager, possibly late in the 1820s, Edmund Kean, 1787-1833, the most electrifying actor of his day, of whom Coleridge wrote that watching him act was like seeing Shakespeare by flashes of lightning, came to Buxton for one night, en route for Manchester. Thornhill persuaded him to act Richard III, his greatest part, promising him half the receipts. Kean agreed and performed to a crowded house. When Thornhill offered him the promised share of the box office receipts next morning, Kean declined:

> Mr Thornhill you are welcome to my services; I shall not accept of any remuneration, for this reason - you have ten children - I have only one.

An appealing story! Kean of all actors knew the rigours of unsuccessful theatricals. After an incredibly harsh childhood, he tramped the country with his wife and two sons (until the elder died), suffering the terrible trials of life as a strolling player. On 26 January 1814 he played Shylock at Drury Lane to loud acclaim, and went on to further meteoric successes. Imagine the excitement in Buxton when it was known that this actor was in town!

The playbill for a performance of *Broken Sword* in 1819 shows that four Thornhills were in the cast: Master C., Mr G., Miss and Miss E. Others in the company were Mr Daniels, Mrs Davis, Mr Hall, Mr and Miss Peirce, Mr and Mrs Platt, Miss Shuter, Mr Slaney, Mr and Mrs Smythson. After the play Mr Daniels sang and the two

Playbill for The Broken Sword at Buxton, October 21, 1819.

Thornhill girls gave a rural dance. We learn that the Thornhills lived "at the Thespian Cottage adjoining the Theatre" and that tickets could be obtained there as well as at Mr Moore's at the Post Office in the Crescent.

There is a remarkable consistency in prices shown on the playbills over a considerable span of years: three shillings for the Boxes, two shillings for the Pit and one shilling for the Gallery. Two playbills for 1804 give boxes 4s, Pit 2s 6d, Gallery 1s 6d, with a second price of 1s for the Gallery if the playgoer waited until the end of the second act; but bills for the New Theatre dated 1834 show the lower prices of 3s, 2s, 1s; the same prices were charged at the Richmond Theatre in Yorkshire. The English are notoriously mean about theatre tickets. The most celebrated example of their reluctance to pay the economic rate was the alarming, long sustained battle at Covent Garden in 1809. After the fire of September 1808, in which twenty-three firemen lost their lives, the theatre was quickly rebuilt at vast expense. It re-opened within the year and John Philip Kemble[9] raised the prices. The famous OP (Old Prices) riots broke out; as Kemble stepped forward to speak on the opening night (the plays were *Macbeth* and *The Quaker*) there was uproar in the house. Loud cries of "Old Prices!" drowned Kemble's attempts. The police and soldiers were called, the Riot Act read out, but the noise continued and was repeated every night for sixty-one nights before Kemble gave way.

Since higher prices appear on some surviving Buxton playbills, are we to assume that OP riots here brought them down again? Surely not, in a theatre regularly filled by a genteel audience...

It is not clear when the Theatre closed or was demolished, but what is clear is that the Thornhill family continued to be prominent in management and performance when Buxton could boast a New Theatre early in the 1830s.

Detail from a caricature of Edmund Kean (1787-1833) of Drury Lane, performing Shakespeare's Richard III, the role he performed once in Buxton sometime in the 1820s.

---

[9] John Philip Kemble 1757-1823, eldest son of a famous theatrical family. The great Sarah Siddons was his sister. Kemble was a grave, formal actor, considered best in tragic parts. Successively manager of Drury Lane and Covent Garden theatres, he suffered financially and had to sell his splendid library. The Sixth Duke of Devonshire bought it for £2,000. The 700 volumes of plays included the first four Shakespeare folios and thirty nine quartos.

Hall Bank, Buxton. The date 1862 has been inserted on an engraving made at an earlier date. By 1862 the two establishments to the right of the Hall Bank houses, and opposite the Old Hall, had been demolished and Broad Walk established. Those two establishments are often mistakenly identified as the second Buxton theatre. The theatre actually stood beyond the building nearer to Hall Bank. The Tithe Map of 1848 (next page) makes this clear.

CHAPTER THREE
A Grand Place

REMINISCENCES by old Buxtonians of the 1830s, 40s, 50s and later, printed in the Buxton *Herald* in 1905, almost sixty three years after the paper first appeared, give glimpses of the New Theatre at the bottom of Hall Bank. To one it was a jewel, a

> bijou theatre, with frequent visits of the "stars" of the London theatres;

to John Owen of Broad Walk, who had served at the Old Hall and Errwood Hall in his youth, it was a strange and wonderful place. He remembered

> when quite a boy, going into the theatre at the bottom of Hall Bank[1] - I don't think I paid anything as I had no money, and I did think what a grand place it was. The theatre was only open about three months in the summer.

Such unaffected accounts stir the blood in a way the guide books never do. Here is Rhodes's description in his *Derbyshire Tourists Guide* (1837):

> At the west end of the Crescent, nearly opposite The Hall, is Billinge's Billiard Room[2], a great accommodation in such a place as Buxton, where the weather sometimes urges to indoor amusements; and close behind the Billiard Room is the Theatre - a small place, but neat and convenient within, and occupied, during the season, by a very respectable company of comedians.

We must be grateful for the detail Rhodes gives of the position of the Theatre. The Buxton Tithe Map of 1848 reinforces his words. Land allotments are numbered. The

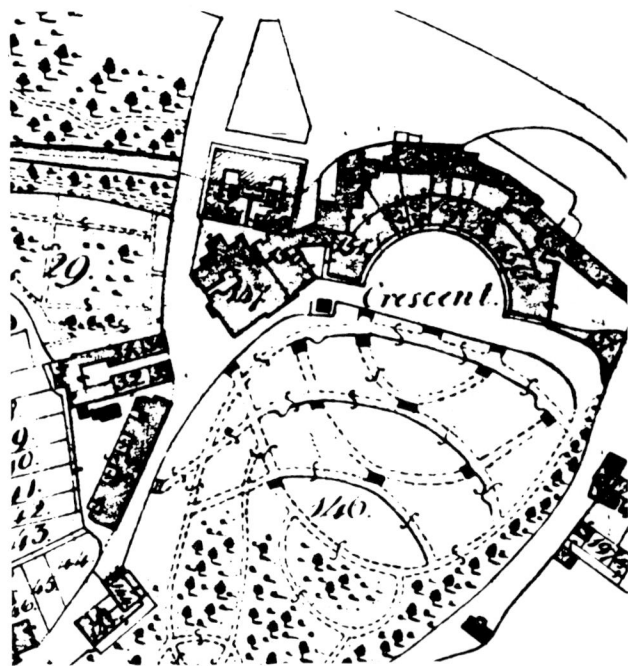

Part of the Diocese of Derby Buxton Tithe map 1848. Directly opposite the Old Hall Hotel No 30 is the Billiard Room, No 32 is the Theatre. Note that Broad Walk and Hartington Road were not yet established.

key gives names of occupiers and types of buildings. The elongated, horse-shoe-shaped group opposite the Old Hall, west of the Crescent, shows

No 30   Mary E Bates - Billiard Room - 2 perches
No 31   Mary Bates - Stables, yards and coach houses 32 perches
No 32   John Capel - The Theatre - 6 perches
No 33   William Smith - House and Shop - 4 perches

The owner of the land upon which these buildings stood,

---

[1] Broad Walk and Hartington Road were not then in existence.
[2] A note on Peter Potter's map of Buxton, 1803, at Chatsworth, locates Billinge's Billiard Room near Cavendish Circus, beyond the George. Jewitt tells us that Buxton had three billiard tables in the 1800s, but he, like Rhodes, locates Billinge's near the Hall. Chatsworth accounts refer to the one near the Hall as the Old Billiard Room.

Extract from Chatsworth accounts for 1854. Items 217 and 226 refer to demolition of the second Buxton Theatre on what is now Broad Walk.

of course, was the Sixth Duke of Devonshire. Mary Bates, No 31, was the occupier of the Old Hall Hotel, and the buildings at the foot of Hall Bank provided not only stables and coach house, but two places of amusement for guests, conveniently near: a billiard room and a theatre.

A Chatsworth map of the township of Buxton, dated 1853, and Sir Joseph Paxton's map of 1854 show those buildings still in situ, and entries in terriers and valuation records at Chatsworth leave us in no doubt that the Sixth Duke maintained the theatre for the town, as he did so much else. Whilst no record of the actual building or adaptation of this theatre has so far come to light, hours of searching through leather-bound ledgers, stored from floor to ceiling in a fascinating cupboard at Chatsworth, produced this intriguing item:

1851
September 26
To S. & J. Turner for carpenter's work at the
Theatre .... 18s.10d.

Later searches[3] produced evidence of further expenditure:-

1852
July 20 Paid Sarah Littlewood for cleaning the
Theatre .... 15s.10d.
July 28 Paid R. F. Smith for painting the
Theatre .... £10.0.0.

[3] These were made by Mr Hugo Read, CBE, whose help has been invaluable.

Extract from Chatsworth accounts: Arrears at Lady Day 1851. The fifth item shows John Capel (Caple) a bad tenant of the Theatre. Did his non-payment of rent hasten demolition in 1854?

And on 31 December of that same year, 1852, there was a sudden flurry of work and expenditure:

S. & J. Turner were paid £5.7s.10d. for more carpenter's work; Thomas Flint received £3.7s.0. for drapery for the Theatre and M. Y. Colquhoun received the considerable sum of £90 for gas fittings at the Baths, Ball Room, St. Ann's Hotel, Theatre, Offices and News Room. The following year, 1853, expenditure on the Theatre appears to have been restricted to 4s.11d. for unspecified repairs by John Kitchen; there was considerable work done at the Shakespeare Inn, however.

On 30 September 1854, we read

Paid John Blunt & Company for labour in pulling down the Theatre .... £3.8s.9d.

and on 14 October Edmund Yeomans is recorded as receiving £5.3s.0d. for labour for the same undertaking. Later references and payments concerning this demolition work leave us in no doubt that the town lost this second theatre five years or so before the present Broad Walk was established. Perhaps destruction of the Theatre was undertaken because John Capel (or Caple), the tenant, did not pay his rent. As early as 1851, Chatsworth accounts reveal:

Arrears due at Lady Day
The Theatre (Caple, John) bad .... £20.0.0.

and under Buxton 1852 appears the following:

Variations in the Rental to Lady Day 1852
The Theatre .... £20.0.0.

The Rent is taken out of the Rental and will henceforth be accounted for in the second statement if any should arise.

The Duke's agent appears to be accepting that there is little hope of payment from this bad tenant.

From the exquisitely penned valuation of the Sixth Duke's estate in Buxton, made by John Bromley of Derby in 1855, we learn that the Theatre occupied six perches, the Billiard Room two perches, the house opposite the Hall four perches and the Hall stables, yard and coach house 32 perches[4], all corroborating the information given on the 1848 tithe map. House, billiard room and theatre are listed as being "in hand" in 1855; in other words, they were no longer tenanted.

As with the Spring Gardens Theatre, so with the Theatre at the foot of Hall Bank: no single picture of it has come to light. Many people, the admirable Ernest Axon[5] among them, wrongly assume the Theatre to be one of two small buildings, to the right of the first house at the foot of Hall Bank, opposite the Hall, depicted on several general views of Buxton which date from the early and middle 1800s. The 1803, 1848 and 1853 maps show that assumption to be incorrect. Those buildings were the Billiard Room and a house-and-shop. Just beyond those two, on the engraving enclosed within a circle, entitled *A View of Buxton with the Improvements from the Grove*, is a small building, dimly discernible. Presumably that is the Theatre, John Owen's "grand place", labelled "New" on the 1834 Buxton playbills which have survived. It does not look very prepossessing, but appears to have been considered some improvement on the "Old" Theatre.

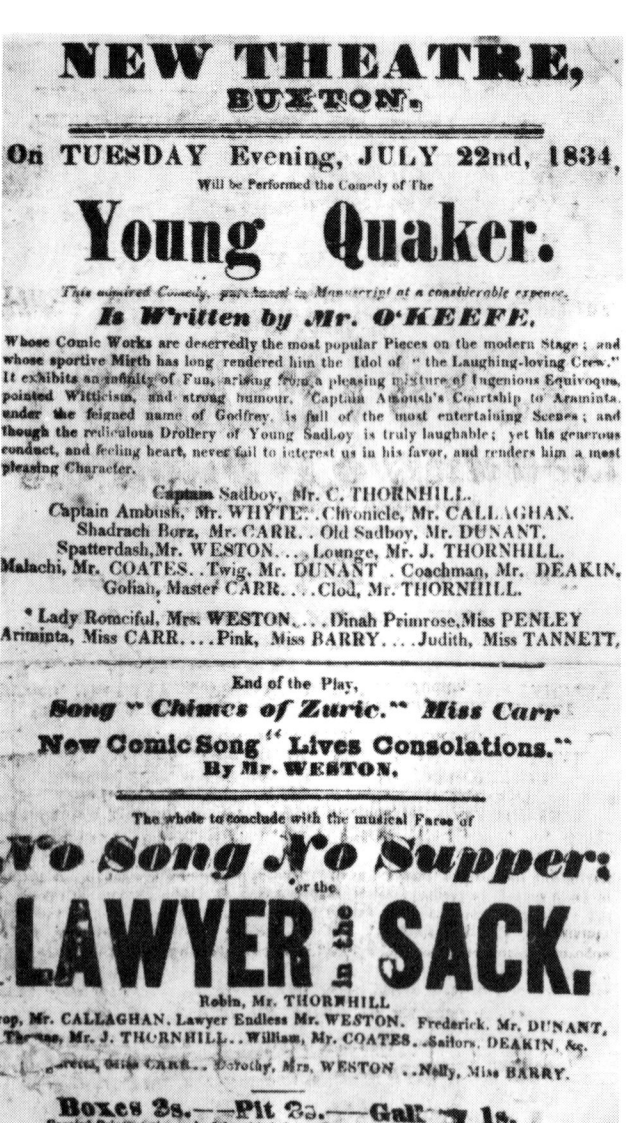

Playbill for The Young Quaker at the New Theatre, Buxton, July 22 1834.

[4] One rod, pole or perch = 5½ yards.
[5] Ernest Axon, FSA, Deputy Librarian of Manchester Public Libraries, lived in Buxton for over twenty years. He gave a series of papers to Buxton Archeological Society in the 1930s. They were reprinted in the *Advertiser* and are required reading for anyone interested in the history of Buxton.

A View of Buxton with the Improvements from the Grove. A somewhat teasing picture but it gives what may be a glimpse of the theatre at the foot of Hall Bank, opposite the Old Hall. Hall Bank houses are represented at the top of the picture. To the right, below them, a small building is dimly discernible, representing either the coach house of the Old Hall or the New Theatre. See p29 1848 Tithe Map No 32.

The "Special Commissioner", collecting reminiscences for the *Herald* in 1905, heads one article.

The Play's the Thing and begins:

> The first playhouse or theatre in Buxton was situated in Church-street[6], from which one would gather that the requirements of theatre-goers in those days were easily satisfied. This was succeeded by one of more commodious character on the site now occupied by Messrs J. Milligan & Sons ... and a still later Temple of Thespis on an even more pretentious scale was erected at the corner of Broad Walk facing the Old Hall Hotel.

We cannot be sure precisely when the Spring Gardens Theatre was abandoned in favour of the "New" Theatre opposite the Hall. Surviving playbills of 1834 announce plays to be performed at the "New" Theatre that year, and we know that the famous violinist, Nicolo Paganini, performed there on one night in the Autumn of 1833.[7] That was a thrilling occasion. Seat prices were raised considerably; even so, the house overflowed. People came from all parts of the county, vying for whatever seats they could obtain:

> Mr Wm Johnson's father being granted admission on payment of half a guinea, this being regarded as a special favour due to the fact of him being a musician. (Buxton *Herald*.)

Presumably the move to the New Theatre took place at the beginning of the 1830s. From the Buxton *Herald* we learn that "respectable" though the company at the New Theatre was, clumsy mishaps occasionally marred performances. One of these occurred when Mr William Perkins was engaged to stand in the wings and play his clarinet off stage, synchronising his notes with those of an actor on stage

> the delusion being kept up by the actor also having an

---

[6] No other references to a theatre in Church Street survive. Ernest Axon discounts the possibility of a theatre so far from the fashionable part of Buxton.

[7] Nicolo Paganini 1782-1840. Violinist and composer of demonic quality and intensity, popularly believed to be inspired by the Devil!

BY DESIRE,

NEW THEATRE BUXTON.

Mr. C. THORNHILL has great pleasure in announcing to the Nobility, Gentry and Inhabitants of Buxton, that he has concluded an Engagement with **Mr. Meadows, from the Theatre Royal, Covent Garden** FOR THREE NIGHTS ONLY.

On TUESDAY Evening, September 2nd, 1834

Will be Performed the celebrated Comedy of The

SCHOOL OF REFORM;

Or, How to Rule a Husband.

Bob Tyke, M. MEADOWS.

Lord Avondale, Mr. WHYTE....Mr. Ferment, Mr. C. THORNHILL.
General Tarragon....Mr. CALLAGHAN.
Frederic, Mr. CARR....Old Man, Mr. TANNETT
Bailiff, Mr. DEAKIN....Timothy, Mr WESTON.
Peter, Mr. J. THORNHILL.
Mrs. Ferment, Miss PENLEY....Mrs. St. Clair, Miss BARRY.
Julia, Miss CARR......Shelah, Miss TANNETT
Mrs. Nicely, Miss WESTON.

End of the Play.

A Comic Song, by Mr. Weston.
Song by Miss CARR.
Comic Dance, by Mr. J. THORNHILL

To conclude with the

SECRET.

Dupuis, Mr. CARR...Valere, Mr. DUNNANT...Thomas, Mr. MEADOWS.
Porter Mr. COATES.
Mrs Dupis Mrs. HARDING...Angelica, Miss CARR.

Boxes 3s. — Pit 2s. — Gallery 1s.
Second Price at the end of the third Act. Boxes 2s—Pit, 1s. 6d—Gallery, 6d.
Doors opened at half past 6 o'clock and the curtain to rise precisely at 7

Two playbills for performances by Drinkwater Meadows of Covent Garden theatre. He starred in Buxton for three nights in the week beginning Tuesday 2 September 1834.

> **NEW THEATRE**
> BUXTON.
>
> **FOR THE BENEFIT OF**
> *Mr MEADOWS*
> OF THE THEATRE ROYAL, COVENT GARDEN,
> And last Night of his performing here.
>
> On SATURDAY Evening, September 6th, 1834
> Will be presented the very Popular Musical Play of
>
> **ROB ROY?**
> OR,
> *Auld Lang Syne.*
>
> Bailie Nicol Jarvie - - - Mr. Meadows.
> Rob Roy Macgregor Campbell, Mr CARR.
> Sir Frederick Vernon..............Mr TANNETT.
> Rashleigh Osbaldistone..Mr. WHYTE.
> Francis Osbaldistone.. Mr. C. THORNHILL—Hamish..Miss ——
> Captain Thornton..Mr, DUNANT—Major Galbraith..Mr. THORNHILL.
> Mc. Stuart.. Mr. J. THORNHILL—Owen, Mr, CALLAGHAN.
> Saunders Wylie..Mr. COATES—Dougal..Mr. WESTON.
> Helen Macgregor Campbell..Miss PENLEY.
> Diana Vernon..Miss CARR—Mattie. Mrs. WESTON.
> Jean Mac Alpine....Miss TANNETT——Martha....Miss BARRY.
>
> **A Comic Song, by Mr. Weston.**
>
> In the course of the evening, and incidental to the Piece, an *entirely New Scene* of
> **ROMANTIC VIEWS in the HIGHLANDS,**
> Will be introduced, painted expressly for this occasion, by Mr. E. Drennan.
>
> To conclude with Kerme'ys admired Farce of The
> **Illustrious Stranger**
> OR,
> **BURIED ALIVE.**
>
> Benjamin Bowball . . Mr. MEADOWS.
> Aboulifar, Mr. CARR..Azan, Mr. WESTON . Alibajon, Mr. TANTNET.
> Gimbo, Mr. WHYTE..High Priest, Mr. COATES.
> Officers, Mr. DUNANT and Mr. J. THORNHILL.
> Irza, Miss CARR..Fatima, Miss BARRY..Officers, Guards, Nobles, &c.
>
> **Boxes 3s. —Pit 2s.— Gallery 1s.**
> Second Price at the end of the third Act. Boxes 2s.—Pit, 1s. 6d.—Gallery, 6d.
> Doors opened at half past 6 o'clock and the curtain to rise precisely at 7
> Tickets and places for the Boxes may be had at the Library, at the Hotels,
> Eagle, Angel Cheshire Cheese, Kings Head; and of Mr. Thornhill, at the
> Theatre, from ten until two o'clock
>
> S. DODGE, PRINTER, STOCKPORT.

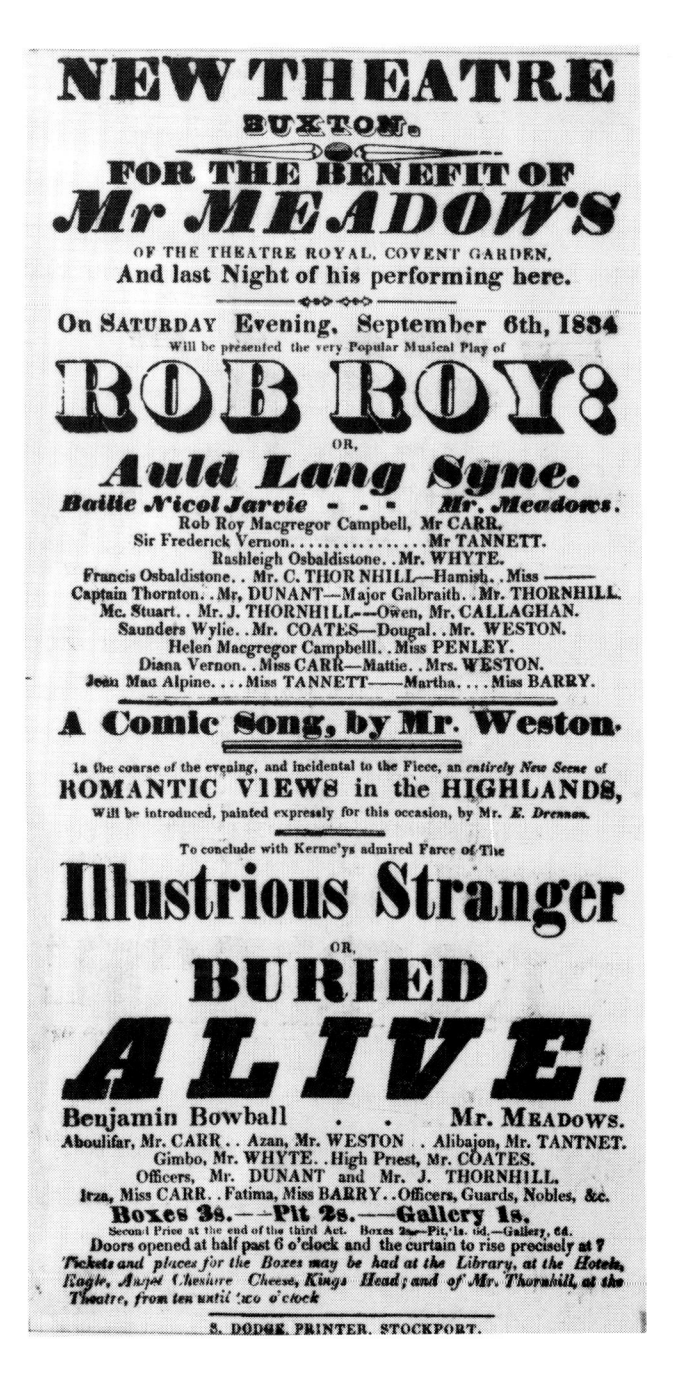

instrument and going through the motions of playing. One night Mr Perkins's attention was taken up with something transpiring at the back part of the stage, and instead of keeping an eye on the actor and stopping playing when the latter took the instrument from his mouth, he kept on discoursing sweet music for all he was worth, the actor having to turn, as best he might, the outburst of laughter the incongruity of the situation provoked.

The name Thornhill features prominently in the playbills:

> Mr C. Thornhill announces to the Nobility, Gentry and Inhabitants of Buxton that he has concluded an Engagement with Mr Meadows, from the Theatre Royal, Covent Garden, for three nights only.

It becomes mildly diverting to count the number of Thornhills (or Thornills as the name appears on the family gravestone in St. Anne's churchyard) included in the company for any given play. The Mr Meadows named above was Drinkwater Meadows, one of a number of London performers who came to perform in Buxton during the Summer months when the London theatres were dark. Mr Meadows performed here on September 2, 4 and 6 in 1834. He gave seven of his favourite parts. Imagine the fierce activity necessary on the part of the prompter as the members of the local company strove to retain their lines in seven plays in one week!

The playbill for July 22, 1834, announces the performance of *The Young Quaker*. This "admired comedy, purchased in manuscript at a considerable expense" was the work of John O'Keefe.[8] Mr C. Thornhill headed the cast. Others in the company are Messrs Whyte, Callaghan, Carr, Dunant, Weston, J. Thornhill, Coates, Deakin, Thornhill, Master Carr, Mrs Weston and Misses Penley, Carr, Barry and Tannett. Old prices prevail: 3s, 2s, 1s, but second prices are advertised at the end of the third Act - Boxes 2s, Pit 1s 6d, Gallery 6d. It is good to see that local subjects were celebrated. The

---

[8] John O'Keefe, 1747-1833, actor and later, playwright. He wrote prolifically: light-hearted plays, farces, pantomimes and comic operas. He became blind in his late twenties, alas.

playbill for 15 August 1837 tells us that *Poole the Outlaw*[9] is

> An entirely new romantic and historical play (in three acts) founded on legends and traditions connected with Buxton and its vicinity .. Expressly written and adapted to dramatic representation for this Theatre, with a new prologue and epilogue by Mr Charles Bass.

The play was presented "By desire of the Ladies and Gentlemen at the Grove" and its scenes included "the Ancient Hall of Buxton as it appeared in 1550... The Lovers Leap with distant view of Mill-Dale ... John O'Gaunt's Rock &c &c ... The Terrace Gardens of the Hall of Buxton ... Poole's Hole ... View of Haddon Hall ... The River Wye in a Torrent - Dreadful Storm ... Chatsworth House and Park". It is to be hoped that the New Theatre had a strong scene painter to cope with representations of those! There were four Thornhills in the company: Mr C., Mr and Mrs J., and Miss. Only two other names from the 1834 company are included: Deakin and Weston. The new names are: Messrs Bass, Dyott, Herbert, M'Gregor, Montague, Neville, Thomas, Mrs Dyott, Mrs Montague, Mrs and Miss Neville.

It seems likely that the Mr Deakin mentioned was William Deakin, a member of the Duke's Band, as was William Perkins, the culprit in the clarinet-playing episode. Several stories of Mr Perkins's love of alcohol appear in the *Herald* articles. 1837 was the year of Queen Victoria's accession to the throne. There were celebrations in Buxton for her coronation, and the Band was much in evidence.

> There were tables set all around the Crescent laden with plum puddings, rounds of beef etc., Then they let us young ones to the table, and cut us lumps off, and gave each of us half a gill of beer - we could have drunk a whole gill if they had given it to us. There were bands of music, and the late Mr William Perkins and his company, all of whom were fit to be sent from home[10]....

> The only streets in Buxton then were High-street and Spring-gardens. There was not a house above St. John's Church, except the old Nithen End cottages. It was all fields right away up to the back of the Queen's Head, Eagle Hotel and Hall Bank. It was the same on the east side, fields right up to the Cheshire Cheese and Sun Inn. There was no Quadrant; the Crescent was enclosed (with) cast iron railing, and there was no road, only round by St. John's Church. (Buxton *Herald*.)

Accounts at Chatsworth for the Duke's Band in 1858 show that £318.3.8 was expended on wages, music and repair of instruments. Wages amounted to £31 every two weeks; £13.17.0 was spent on music. The Duke's subscription was £200; hotels, inns and boarding houses contributed £26.1.2 and £58.15.5 came from a voluntary rate collected from local shops. A note at the foot of the page states

> A many objected to pay this rate and some who paid the present rate objected to pay in future.

Mr Irving (clarinet and harp) was bandmaster. Other members were: Mr Edward Johnson, the musician who managed to get a seat to hear Paganini (French horn and violin), Mr William Deakin (cornet), Mr William Perkins (clarinet), Mr William Smith (bassoon and double bass), Mr Wm Pidcock (trombone), Mr Wm Johnson (French horn and violin), Mr Jas Pearson (orpheclide), Mr Wm Sutton (clarinet), Mr W. H. Pidcock (flute), Mr Samuel Percival (flute), and Mr John Goodwin (drum).

Concert Place was so named because Mr Irving lived there. Members of the band used to call on him and they rehearsed at his house.

> So musical were the Buxtonians of those early days that Mr Irving was wont to remark that he could kick music out of the streets, but it is not recorded that he ever resorted to that method to recruit his band. *(Buxton Herald.)*

---

[9] Poole's Cave, celebrated in works by Thomas Hobbes and Charles Cotton (friend of Isaak Walton), was one of the famous seven "Wonders of the Peak" all tourists felt compelled to visit when they came to Buxton.

[10] A euphemism for "drunk".

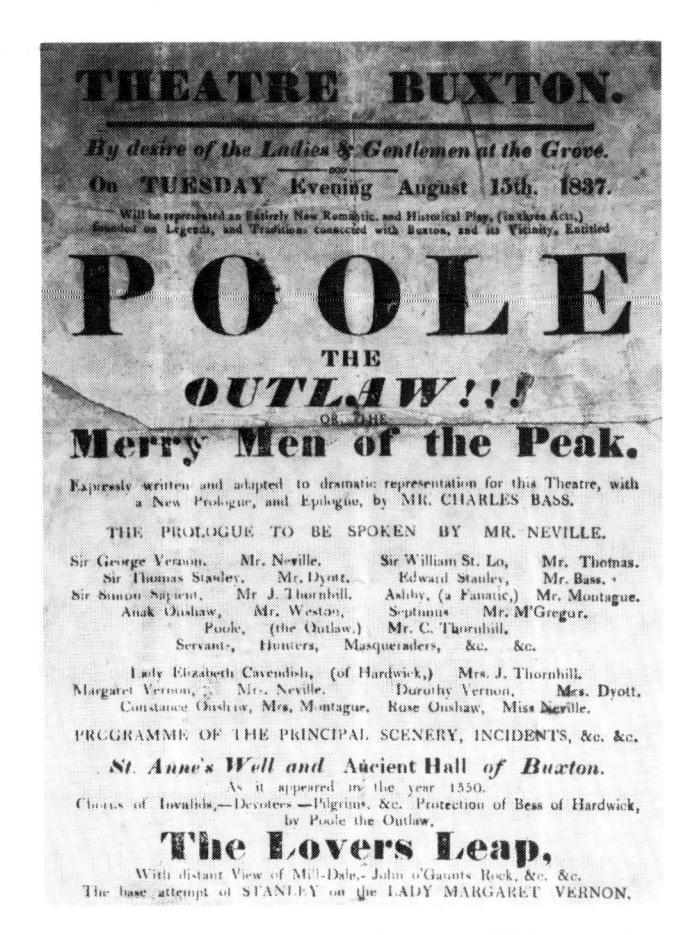

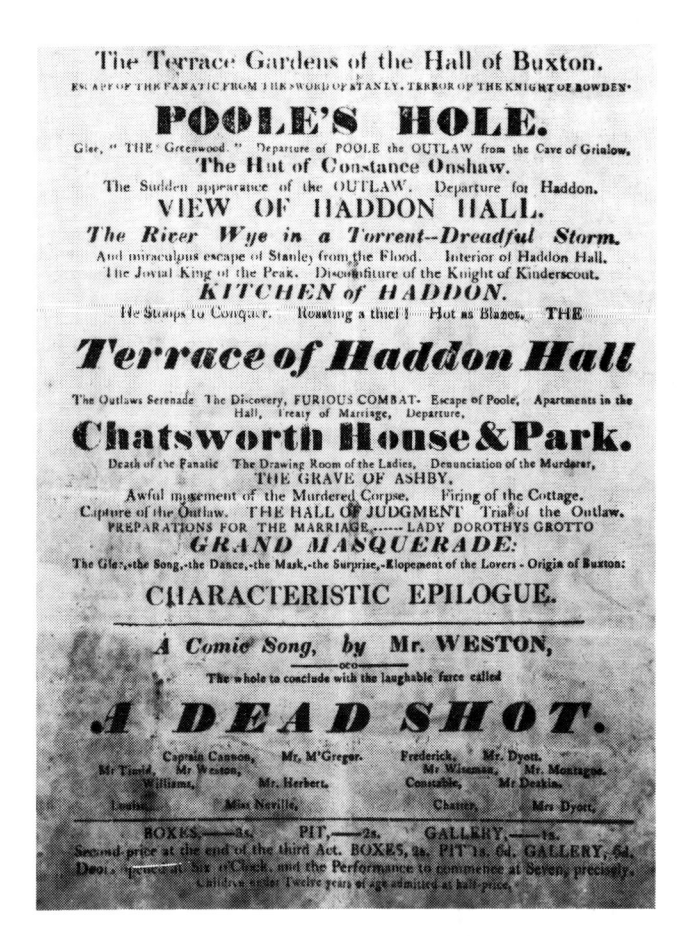

Two sections of a large playbill for a performance of a play with local connotations for Buxton: Poole the Outlaw, presented on August 15 1837.

There are no references to an orchestra at the Theatre, yet we see from playbills that songs and dances were performed as well as plays. Presumably the Duke's Band served as orchestra, or supplied one or two musicians whenever the Theatre needed them.

After the demolition of the Theatre, starting in 1854, the Band no doubt assumed even greater importance than before. No spa can expect to prosper which fails to provide entertainment for visitors. A "boom" period was imminent for Buxton. The arrival of the railway in 1863 occasioned much building of houses and hotels. The town was to be left without a theatre for 35 years but theatrical activity certainly continued throughout that time. "Set-up" arrangements were the order of the day. Buxton Museum has a collection of bills and programmes showing us that various locations were used: the Court House, the Assembly Room - any convenient space, in

Entertainment in Buxton before the Pavilion Gardens building opened in 1871. The Duke's Band, resplendent in "blueish" - coloured uniform with a "plenitude of small silver buttons", is depicted around the Duke's bandstand, a portable, umbrella-like wooden structure.

short, where performers and audience could be accommodated under one roof. Not until 1889 did the town again boast a building set aside specifically for theatre.

Meanwhile, the Duke's Band played on, resplendent in uniform "of a blue-ish colour ... ornamented with a plenitude of small silver buttons." The musicians stood round the Duke's band-stand, a picturesque, portable wooden structure with umbrella-like roof. It afforded no protection in bad weather, but the musicians were hardy creatures, always in good humour, and Buxton was amply endowed with inns to which they resorted quite regularly:

> Of the Buxton old band, old Goodwin was drummer,
> They always were thirsty, both winter & summer;
> They have played many a time in our old cot!
> And never in this world was there a merrier lot.[11]

11 Included in a letter to the *Herald*, February 1905, from Mr John Buxton.

CHAPTER FOUR
The Entertainment Stage

THE Sixth Duke of Devonshire, the beloved Bachelor Duke, died at Hardwick Hall a little after six on Monday morning, 18 January 1858. All Derbyshire was plunged into mourning. Buxton was especially stricken. Mr John Roberts, veteran newsagent of Terrace Road in 1905, wrote to the *Buxton Herald:*

> ...The Duke's death was, as may well be imagined, a great loss to Buxton.

Great changes followed. Mr Roberts continues:

> ...the Buxton estate was administered on more commercial lines. The expenses connected with the band, the maintenance of the Hall Bank, the Square, the Hall gardens, and Serpentine were discontinued, and the Duke made a most generous offer to a company, to be called the Buxton Gardens and Improvement Company,[1] of the land occupied by the then free Hall Gardens and Serpentine, as far as the Burlington Road, and the fields of that portion of the Gardens between Broad Walk and Burlington Road, at a merely nominal rent. To my mind it should have been made to the town instead of to a company.[2] Its formation, however, has been of the greatest possible benefit to the town, and also beneficial to the shareholders, and every right-thinking individual will wish it may long continue so, and that its management in the future will be equal to that in the past.

The Seventh Duke, William (1808-1891), the former Lord Burlington, thus initiated exercises in self-help in Buxton, a town where

> the result of the Sixth Duke's generosity was an entire absence of initiative in the village and put a premium on lazy indifference.[3]

Fortunately there were private individuals who had sufficient vigour and initiative to risk their own money in the town's best interests. In fairness to the "villagers" it

William, Seventh Duke of Devonshire (1808-1891).

should be pointed out that ducal splendour had not been sought; it had been given to the locality, mainly so that the marvellous gift of the waters might be exploited and Buxton made fashionable. No doubt unambitious

---

[1] 1871-1889 Buxton Improvements Company: 1889-1927 Buxton Gardens Company. Mr Roberts, somewhat elderly in 1905, is telescoping the two phases of the Company.

[2] The town acquired all the Company's properties in 1927 for a very low figure.

[3] Robert Grundy Heape: Buxton under the Dukes of Devonshire 1948.

villagers would have been content to have kept the place to themselves, with all its lack of amenities. The spirit which led to a petition to Elizabeth I, complaining of the expense to inhabitants caused by the numbers of sick and lame persons coming to Buxton from afar to take the waters, lingers on in Mr John Roberts's recollections of the 1840s:

> we had no large debt on the town, no expensive establishment to keep up, no district rate, no water rate, very few "monkeys" on the chimneys, no lawyers, no policemen, no income tax to pay when you had no income, no Town Council to spend that which we had not got and to leave a debt to posterity and thus make life a struggle.

What they did have was a generous, all-providing Duke who maintained the elegance his father had brought to a part of Buxton, so that fashionable people crowded the place during the season, giving it an animation and variety it would never itself have generated. What the town now had in the Seventh Duke was a fine mathematical brain,[4] one who could read a balance sheet and guide the townsfolk into developing for themselves the gifts which had been showered upon them.

The Prospectus and Form of Application for Shares of the Buxton Improvements Company, December 1869, makes the objects of the company clear:

> to add to the attractions and increase the prosperity of Buxton.

The Company proposed providing enclosed gardens, a covered promenade, a Hall for amusements and recreations, where the Band could perform whatever the weather, the whole to be surrounded by ornamental and well-kept gardens and pleasure grounds.[5] The Duke of Devonshire had undertaken to subscribe half the required capital and had allotted to the Company nine acres of "excellent garden ground",[6] centrally situated in the Hall Gardens, with a portion of the River Wye and part of the lakes and plantations known as the Hall Gardens Ornamental Waters and the Serpentine or Winding Walks, to be held in perpetuity on condition that they were used exclusively for the purposes of such gardens and pleasure grounds. Edward Milner, eminent landscape gardener, was appointed, and the Gardens opened on 11 May 1871. The Pavilion was in use from the second week in August of that year. Once launched, the Company steadily enhanced its holdings, constantly putting more capital into the venture, and faithfully paying the annual dividend of 5 per cent. The Concert Hall[7] was opened in August 1876, providing the town with a splendid hall for musical and theatrical activities, and more and more acres of ground were added as time went by.

The town at this time did not boast a theatre, yet there was plainly an interest in dramatic entertainment. On October 7, 1871, this intriguing notice had appeared in the *Buxton Advertiser*:

> Theatre Royal, Spring Gardens, Buxton.
> Under the management of Mr Henry Mandeville.
> Licensed to play pieces of the Dramatic Authors.
> This theatre being now duly licensed
> according to Act of Parliament, will
> OPEN FOR THE SEASON TONIGHT,
> with a full and efficient company with
> DRAMA, COMEDY and FARCE
>
> Stage manager Mr J. Rooke.
> Reserved stalls 2s Pit stalls 1s Area 6d.
> Children in arms one guinea.

Under the headline *The New Theatre in Spring Gardens*, the *Advertiser* published these sympathetic words:

> ...The old independent chapel in Spring Gardens is

---

[4] The Seventh Duke, formerly Lord Burlington: He was placed Second Wrangler in the highly competitive and rigorous mathematical examinations at Cambridge and high in the Classical tripos. He was a man of formidable intellect and equally formidable shyness and reserve. John Pearson quotes Lord Esher's description: "His bowed figure tacked into a room like a vessel finding an intricate channel." His marriage to Blanche Howard, niece of the Sixth Duke, appears to have been very happy. She died in 1840, aged 28. Her husband mourned her loss to the end of his days. The Sixth Duke's inscription in the Painted Hall at Chatsworth refers to her death "in the year of his sorrow!"

[5] The iron railings enclosing the Gardens were not removed until November 1976. Dove Holes Cricket Club bought some of them to fence off their ground.

[6] Estimated value of the ground: £1,000 per acre.

[7] Known to us now as The Octagon.

Pavilion Gardens, Buxton in the late 1870s. The Buxton Improvements Company, beginning in 1871, provided the elegant glass and iron structures depicted above for the pleasure of Buxton residents and visitors. They stand in the Pavilion Gardens, landscaped by Edward Milner of Sydenham, given by the Seventh Duke of Devonshire on the understanding that the land remained as pleasure ground.

The domed building, left, is the Concert Hall (now the Octagon) designed by the Buxton architect R R Duke and opened in 1876.

The central pavilion with spire, designed by Milner, was destroyed by fire in June 1983 and rebuilt a year later. Beyond it, right, is St John's Church, completed 1812, and right of that is a glimpse of the undomed Devonshire Hospital (formerly the Great Stables by John Carr.)

now converted into a Theatre, and the first performance is announced for this evening. This event would have taken place weeks ago but for the legal difficulties and obstructions which poor players have to overcome before they can earn their bread and cheese without fear of the law. If similar difficulties were in the way of joiners, masons, tailors, etc, many a family would have to go on short commons before the law was satisfied. It is difficult to see why players should be subjected to these drawbacks more than others. It is to be hoped, however, now the Theatre is at last opened, that prices will be produced to the profit and credit of the establishment, and the amusement and instruction of the public. We refer our readers to the advertisement, and wish the proprietor good wishes.

The venture appears to have been short lived. A note appeared in the *Advertiser* of 28 October 1871:

> The Manager of the little theatre in Spring Gardens - Mr Mandeville - "skedaddled" on Tuesday last, with everything, as the phrase goes, that "he could lay his hands on", leaving the poor players without their salaries, and the landlord and everybody else connected with the establishment, unsatisfied.[8]

---

[8] A further sad note appeared in the *Advertiser:* This evening and on Monday next, Mrs and Miss Hilling-Montagu (the daughter and granddaughter of the late Mr Thornhill) who were part of the company in the Spring Gardens Theatre, will give an entertainment in the old Town Hall on the Eagle Parade when it is hoped that they will be patronised to an extent that will make up the loss they have sustained by the dishonesty of their late employer.

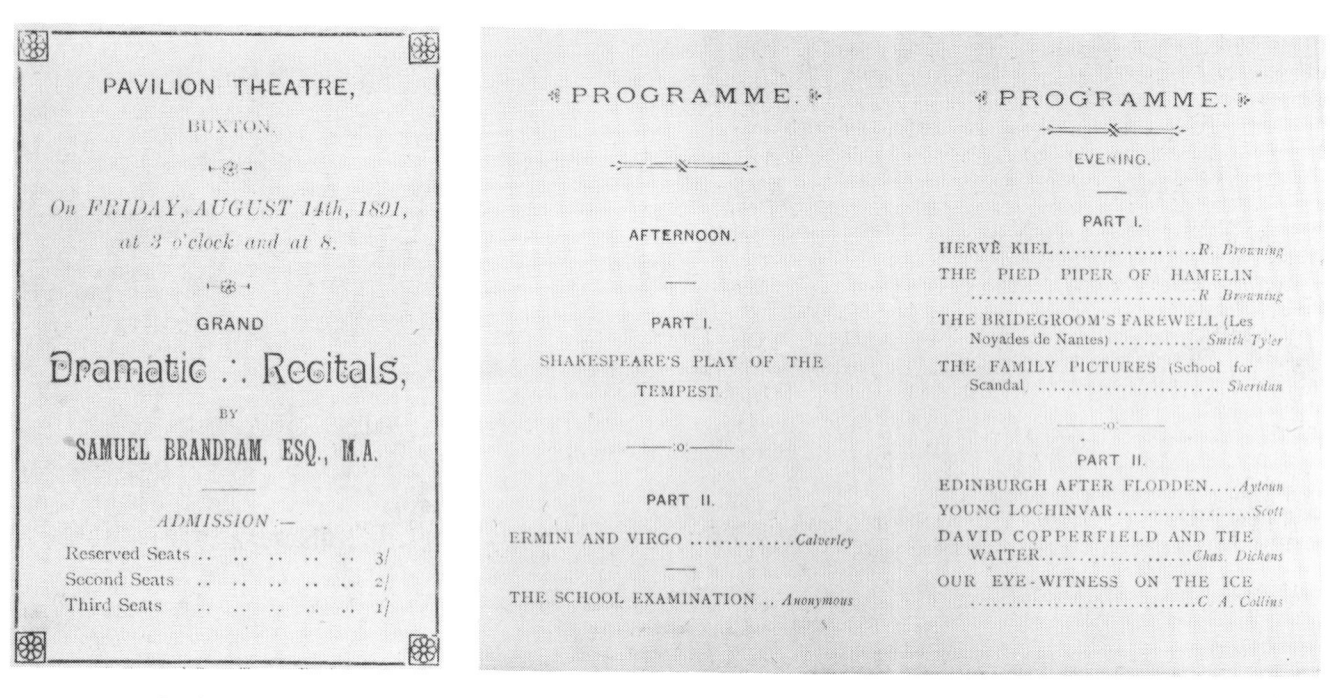

> **PAVILION THEATRE,**
> BUXTON.
>
> On *FRIDAY, AUGUST 14th, 1891,*
> *at 3 o'clock and at 8.*
>
> GRAND
> Dramatic ∴ Recitals,
> BY
> SAMUEL BRANDRAM, ESQ., M.A.
>
> ADMISSION :—
> Reserved Seats 3/
> Second Seats 2/
> Third Seats 1/

> **✻ PROGRAMME. ✻**
>
> AFTERNOON.
>
> PART I.
>
> SHAKESPEARE'S PLAY OF THE
> TEMPEST.
>
> :o:
>
> PART II.
>
> ERMINI AND VIRGO .... *Calverley*
>
> THE SCHOOL EXAMINATION .. *Anonymous*

> **✻ PROGRAMME. ✻**
>
> EVENING.
>
> PART I.
>
> HERVÊ KIEL .... *R. Browning*
> THE PIED PIPER OF HAMELIN
> .... *R Browning*
> THE BRIDEGROOM'S FAREWELL (Les
> Noyades de Nantes) .... *Smith Tyler*
> THE FAMILY PICTURES (School for
> Scandal .... *Sheridan*
>
> :o:
>
> PART II.
>
> EDINBURGH AFTER FLODDEN ....*Aytoun*
> YOUNG LOCHINVAR ....*Scott*
> DAVID COPPERFIELD AND THE
> WAITER................ *Chas. Dickens*
> OUR EYE-WITNESS ON THE ICE
> .... *C A. Collins*

Pavilion Theatre programme 1891, showing how quickly the name of the theatre completed in 1889 was changed from The Entertainment Stage.

Meanwhile, dramatic entertainments[9] were provided in various places in the town and eventually the Directors of the Buxton Improvements Company decided to add a drama space to their existing buildings, siting it next to the Pavilion on St. John's Road. In deference to the wishes of Dr Robertson, Chairman, the space duly provided was referred to as The Entertainment Stage.[10] It was inaugurated by J. L. Toole, bosom friend of the great Victorian actor-manager, Sir Henry Irving. Toole's company was the first to perform upon the new stage, and Toole, with due deference, declared it open in August 1889.[11]

Because the Company was now involved in theatrical entertainment, a change in Articles and Agreements was necessary, and henceforth the Company operated under the name of The Buxton Gardens Company. There were mocking letters and references to the Entertainment Stage for a time in the *Advertiser*. Quite soon it was openly referred to as the New Theatre and eventually, for a number of years, as the Pavilion Theatre. When the Opera House was built, it became the Old Theatre for a time and then was "translated" to become a cinema, the Hippodrome. In 1935, its function as a cinema already superceded (the much more comfortable Opera House, now a cinema, was only a short distance along St John's Road) it was renamed yet again and given a new purpose; it became the Playhouse and was used at first for music and drama festivals, before it became the home of the

[9] Buxton Art Gallery and Museum has a collection of programmes and handbills giving details of some of these entertainments.

[10] Dr Robertson was one of those Victorians for whom the words "theatre" and "eternal damnation" were synonymous.

[11] During this visit, Toole was taken to John Kane's grave in St Anne's churchyard. He was so moved, he paid for the grave to be refurbished.

Anthony Hawtrey (1909-1954) Director of Buxton Repertory Company in the 1940s and 1950s at the Playhouse Theatre.

Buxton Repertory Company. This was undoubtedly the most glorious period in the history of this maid-of-all-work of Buxton theatres. From just after the war (1945) until the restoration of the Opera House in 1979, this theatre provided the town with season after season of live theatrical entertainment. Numerous now well-known actors, directors and designers worked here and all appear to remember their sojourn with great affection. Local amateur companies also regularly presented their work here.

Anthony Hawtrey, son of Sir Charles H. Hawtrey,[12] ran the Embassy Theatre in London for many years, and sent out touring companies from there. Buxton regularly received a Hawtrey tour to provide a repertory season for summer visitors, and sometimes a Christmas show also. Anthony Hawtrey often directed in Buxton, sometimes

J L Toole (1830-1906) actor and manager, who opened the Pavilion Theatre (later the Playhouse) in August 1889.

[12] Sir Charles Hawtrey 1858-1923, old Etonian, son of a master at Eton, he became a very popular actor-manager, with many outstanding successes. A fine light comedy actor, he represented the English gentleman, man-about-town, of his period, with flawless manners, perfect poise and a fine disregard for money. *The Private Secretary* was his most famous success. He was knighted in 1922 for services to the stage.

43

played parts himself. Who could resist a spell in Buxton's bracing air, particularly if hounded in London by all the cares of theatre management? Not only did the Hawtrey seasons give pleasure to summer visitors, they also won a following among Buxtonians themselves. Many people still resident in the town look back upon them, and upon the Playhouse, with great affection and gratitude. Most are still able to recite the names of the actors of those days in a loving litany, many recount tales of personal encounters, and all rejoice when they see those actors now gracing the TV and cinema screens, or treading the boards of London and other stages. Shaun Sutton, Barbara Leslie, Joan Sanderson, Patrick Cargill, Nigel Hawthorne, Gwen Watford, Richard Bebb, Mary Mackenzie, Joss Acland are among many frequently mentioned, but that list is by no means exhaustive.

The collection of Playhouse programmes in Buxton Art Gallery and Museum[13] reveals the debt the town owes to so many playwrights, producers, designers, actors and musicians for untold hours of good, live entertainment.

Theatre is such a splendid unifier in a community. Great though the entertainment and educational values of television are, television does not bring members of a community together and it does not appear to engender the other social gatherings to which theatre so often gives rise. How many people arrange to meet for a drink or a meal together BEFORE watching television? How many choose to get together afterwards to discuss what they have seen? Television so often appears to addle brains, to withdraw people from each other, to empty streets and bars, restaurants and churches. Theatre brings people together, compels them to respond together, seems to encourage them to eat, drink and talk together and to use other places of public resort provided in the locality. In Buxton we are fortunate still to have both possibilities, television and theatre. May it always be so.

What we appear to have lost, at least for the time being, in our theatre, is the steady diet of plays week after week, which our "Cinderella" Playhouse provided for so long. Charles Vance revisited Buxton recently, and reminisced about the seasons he and his company gave at the Playhouse in the early 1960s. He remembers constantly hard work: rehearsing during the day next week's play, performing in the evening this week's play, on Sunday taking to cycles to visit surrounding towns and villages with posters and handbills in the hope of attracting audiences. Shaun Sutton, the present head of BBC TV Shakespeare productions, worked here in several Hawtrey seasons immediately after the last war until the early 1950s. He speaks with complete happiness and affection of those years. Many of the people in the company then are still his friends. His wife, Barbara Leslie, was a member of the company. Several other marriages date from that period and that company. All members submitted to the same rigorous routine: a different play every week. Most declare that they have never worked so hard nor been so happy. They speak gratefully of loyal audiences, the First Nighters Club and so forth, and remember with amusement the efforts of the Pavilion manager of the time, occasionally, to divert Playhouse queues away from the Playhouse Box Office towards the Concert pay box! Aware of the lively interest of the audience, the company organised a weekly competition for the best review written by a member of the audience, of the current play. The prize was two free tickets for the play the following week. Mr Sutton remembers how much Anthony Hawtrey loved to come to Buxton. He was a man of great charm and generosity, and held the company together happily. Mr Sutton pays great tribute also to Mary Purvis who achieved marvels in designing attractive workmanlike sets, week after week, for a stage which no-one could pretend was even remotely ideal.

The list of plays presented in 1951, the sixth season by Hawtrey's company, the Buxton Repertory Company, will give a good indication of what the Playhouse offered during these years after the war and almost up to the time of the restoration of the Opera House: *Castle in the Air, If This Be Error, The Good Young Man, Murder at the Vicarage, High Temperature, Bonaventure, The Ghost*

---

[13] Dr Michael Bishop, Curator, is always delighted to add to the collection. Readers are implored NEVER to destroy a theatre programme, poster or handbill. The Museum will gladly house any that are no longer wanted.

The Hippodrome Cinema, St John's Road, Buxton, the "maid-of-all-work" Buxton theatre. Originally the Entertainment Stage (1889), it was soon dubbed the Pavilion Theatre. After completion of the Opera House it eventually became a cinema. The photograph shows signs of several unattractive alterations to the building. In 1935 it was renamed the Playhouse and is now the Paxton Suite.

Buxton Repertory Company 1948 at the Playhouse: the Company in Emma, an adaptation of Jane Austen's novel.

Train, Travellers Joy, A Murder Has Been Arranged, The Holly and the Ivy, Queen Elizabeth Slept Here, Pick-Up Girl, Charley's Aunt, Mr Bowling Buys a Newspaper, Tovarich, Deliver My Darling, Poison in Jest, School for Spinsters, Fresh Fields, Black Chiffon, Rope, Captain Carvallo, See How They Run.

Many of those plays have sunk without trace; several were current West End successes. Other years, other directors, other companies produced sometimes sterner material - Ibsen and Shaw plays, for example - and gave Buxton samples of the work of J. B. Priestley, Emlyn Williams, St John Ervine, Galsworthy and others. But what feasts of entertainment! And what wonderful training ground for the theatrical profession.

In its last years, the Playhouse was run by Buxton Theatre Arts Trust and local amateur companies performed there. Bob and Nora Burrows and June Dunlevy and their colleagues kept the theatre alive: they moved on to help at the Opera House after the restoration. One of the last occasions for the Playhouse was a happy one: Alan Bates, Derbyshire born actor and star of so many fine plays and films, brought two fellow actors from the National Theatre - Dinsdale Landen and Janet Whiteside - and on Sunday 1 October 1978 they gave a recital to raise money for the Opera House restoration fund. The theatre was full and resounded with affectionate laughter and applause for two or three hours.

After the Opera House reopened, resplendent again, in 1979, "Cinderella" went home. Within a very short period, almost as though a wand had been waved, the Playhouse was no more. It was renovated and re-named the Paxton Suite, and became a multi-purpose hall, operating as a night club, a discotheque, a conference hall, an exhibition centre and, occasionally, an informal drama space.

The name is well chosen, forging another link with the Sixth Duke of Devonshire. Joseph Paxton, 1803-1865, was head gardener at Chatsworth and achieved ultimate fame as Sir Joseph Paxton, designer of the Crystal Palace, 1851.

Buxton Repertory Company 1948: Back row: Charles Williams (manager), Penelope Williams, Liam Gaffney, Jacqueline Barnett, Denis Banyard, Gwen Watford, Joan Sanderson, Gregory Scott. Middle: Shaun Sutton. Front row: Roy Leywood, Mary Mackenzie, Ann Glyn (in front), Patrick Freeman, Barbara Leslie, Will Leighton, Carmen Hill, Margaret Dale (in front), Glenys Cotton.

Gwen Watford and Allan Cuthbertson in The Barretts of Wimpole Street, Buxton Playhouse, 1949.

Patrick Cargill and Julie Mortimer in Cinderella, Buxton Playhouse, 1946.

Above: Arthur Willoughby (1872-1944) first manager of the Opera House, who succeeded his father, John Willoughby, as secretary of the Buxton Gardens Company.

Left: Frank Matcham (1854-1920) prolific theatre architect who designed Buxton Opera House.

Reproduction of the charming coloured cover of the first Opera House programmes, 1903-1907.

The inside pages of the programme for the first play presented at the Opera House, June 1903. Among advertisements it is interesting to see J Milligan & Sons, the emporium built on the site of the first Buxton theatre. The International Stores now occupy the site.

CHAPTER FIVE

A Real Gem[1]

A PARAGRAPH in *The Era* of 12 October 1901 gave information of some significance for Buxton:

> Mr Frank Matcham, the well-known theatrical architect, has returned from his trip through America. In his five weeks' absence from London he has visited New York, Boston, Buffalo, Chicago, Philadelphia, and other towns, and has seen nearly all the principal theatres. His opinion is that there is little to learn from our American cousins in the matter of design and construction of places of amusement, and that certain means of exit employed in the American buildings would certainly not meet with the approval of our London County Council. At the same time there is much to be admired in the order and cleanliness of the buildings, and the attention given to patrons of the theatres as regards their comfort and convenience. Mr Matcham is busily engaged in getting the large and handsome new Empire Palace at Hackney completed for opening next month; also the new Theatre Royal, Newcastle, and the New Hippodrome (the altered Olympia) in that city ready to open at Christmas. The Newcastle Empire is also to be pulled down, and a fine music hall erected on the site and adjoining property from Mr Matcham's designs. Mr Matcham's plans for the new theatre at Buxton have also been approved by the authorities, and his plans for the new Glasgow theatre for Mr Fred Wyndham are now before the Dean of Guild Court.

Frank Matcham, 1854-1920, was the most prolific theatre architect of all time. The number of projects mentioned in the latter part of the paragraph quoted above gives some indication of his industry and expertise. John Willoughby, Secretary of the Buxton Gardens Company and General Manager of the Pavilion Gardens, was wise indeed to engage him for the new theatre for Buxton. Trained under Jethro T. Robinson, consulting architect to the Lord Chamberlain and designer of the Old Vic, Matcham married Robinson's daughter in 1877, and took over his work when Robinson died in 1878. Matcham had prodigious success. This was well deserved; he worked quickly and responsibly, and could be relied upon to complete a contract on time. Whilst his theatre exteriors may not usually have been distinguished, his interiors were lively, sensuous, inexpensive, with technical problems of sight lines, acoustics, space relationships and building materials ably resolved. He was at the peak of his powers in 1901 and Buxton could look forward to a very happy project.

Fashionable London, reading *The Era* on 9 November 1901, learned that Buxton was to have a new theatre:

> "Yes, it is quite true, we have just had a special meeting of the shareholders of the Buxton Gardens Company, and they have unanimously decided upon an expenditure of £25,000 (exclusive of land), with which to build a new theatre and reconstruct the present entrance to the gardens. The plans of Mr Frank Matcham, the prince of playhouse architects, have been approved, and the work will be carried out with as little delay and inconvenience as possible."

The speaker is Mr Arthur Willoughby, the acting-manager of the Buxton Pavilion, an alert gentleman who carries an old head on young shoulders, who seems as charged with energy as an electric battery, and who combines in a happy manner the suaviter in modo with the fortiter in re.[2] The time is a golden October morning of the present year. The sun shines with softened radiance upon one of the most beautiful scenes in all Britain; upon terrace and waterfall, bright flower beds and foliage of many

---

[1] *The Architectural Review* October 1976. Buxton Opera House is listed among surviving provincial theatres of architectural importance: "it is a real gem, inside and out, of Edwardian architecture."

[2] Gently but firmly: with iron hand in velvet glove.

OPERA HOUSE
Pavilion Gardens
OPERA HOUSE
UPPER CIRCLE
DRESS CIRCLE AND STALLS

The Opera House after the 1979 restoration.

*John Willoughby (1838-1916).
A Cornishman, he came to Buxton in the late 1850s. Secretary of the Buxton Improvements (later Gardens) Company and manager of the Pavilion Gardens, he was prime mover in the enterprise of building the Opera House.*

tints, croquet ground, bowling green, and lawn-tennis courts; upon twenty-seven acres of ornamental grounds laid-out by landscape gardeners with green lawns, gay parterres, and varigated shrubberies. Superb forest-trees are reflected in a lake of liquid light. Immediately beyond are the wooded heights, the bold ridges, and the swelling moors of the Derbyshire highlands, making a strikingly diversified sky-line. The place is Mr Willoughby's private office, near the concert hall of the Pavilion; the Crystal Palace of the Peak; and surely no theatrical manager possesses a more pleasantly disposed sanctum. It is a situation that in its romantic picturesqueness makes one think of the doyen of scene-painters, and exclaim, "Bravo, Beverley!"[3] The strains of the morning concert reach the room, which is hung with artistic theatrical posters, and convince the listener that the Buxton Season Band, under the baton of Mr De Jong, is a powerful and artistically blended and balanced orchestra, admirably conducted...

Mr Arthur Willoughby's father, Mr John Willoughby, is known far and wide, at home and away. He is secretary and general manager of the Buxton Gardens Company, and in every way a representative and responsible man. He is chairman of the Buxton School Board. He has been the chairman of the Buxton Urban District Council. He is a churchwarden, and, without being a Pooh-Bah, holds other offices in the Spa of the Peak.

"How long have you been assistant manager?" we ask the son who is walking in his father's footsteps.
"Eight and a-half years."

"Before that?"
"I had five years commercial experience in Manchester, and have found the business training I there received of invaluable assistance in my present post."

"Your theatrical bookings bring you in touch with all the leading companies on tour?"
"With everything that is good on the road."

"And you are associated with the musical engagements at the Pavilion?"
"Yes; we engage Mr De Jong, who provides a season band of no fewer than thirty-two performers. Then there are, independent of that orchestra, organ recitals and pianoforte recitals."

"You have also special concerts?"
"Certainly; and we engage artists like Madame Albani, Madame Adelina Patti, Miss Ada Crossley, Madame Marchesi, Mr Leonard Borwick, Mr Plunket Green, Mr Edward Lloyd, Mr Paderewski, Mr Pachmann, the late Sir Charles and Lady Halle, Mr D'Albert, and Madame Clara Butt."

[3] William Roxby Beverley (1814-89) Distinguished scene painter. He began at the Theatre Royal, Manchester, where his father was manager, but achieved fame during his long association with Drury Lane: 1854 to 1884.

Nearer home, the *Buxton Advertiser* kept the town informed of progress, amidst other vital matters. On 10 January 1903, the Duke and Duchess of Devonshire "accompanied by Miss Muriel Wilson and another lady" visited the town, inspected the new Opera House and lunched at St Ann's Hotel before returning to Chatsworth. Excitement was rising there at the expected visit of King Edward VII and Queen Alexandra. The Volunteers had been warned "to get themselves in readiness to act as a guard of honour" and a "numerous and brilliant house party" was gathering. Amateur theatricals at Chatsworth were in preparation; of Princess Henry of Pless's performance, Buxton learned,

> spectators admired her coolness no less than her acting ... when the prompter did not come to her rescue when her memory failed, looking aside, she peremptorily exclaimed, "Do give me my words"...

But all hopes were dashed with the announcement of the King's influenza. The visit was cancelled. However, the *Advertiser* offered readers consolations: each issue included a lengthy instalment of *The Shadow of Furneaux Chase* by Snowflake, and informed readers that the Post Office in Devonshire Circus was open daily 7am to 9pm, they could "buy five atrocious cigarettes for a penny",[4] and Wheeldons, Fashionable Tailors, 16 High Street, Buxton advertised

> Good looking, Dependable Felts at 2/6, 3/6, 4/6[5]
> How a Man looks depends on his Hat

Early in March, the Annual Report of the Buxton Gardens Company showed that, in spite of a wet summer in 1902 and the cancellation of the Coronation arrangements, sufficient profit had been made to pay shareholders a dividend of 5 per cent, thus preserving its unbroken record of paying dividends each year since the Company began. In the *Advertiser*, *The Shadow of Furneaux Chase* came to a satisfactory conclusion:

> ...and with the divine light of motherhood shining on her lovely face, Lady Reynsford drew her children towards her and kissed them with soft tears.

The Editor felt that March was

> bound to go out like an unblemished lamb this year,

for the storm which commenced on 27 February was, in many parts of the British Isles, such as is only known once or twice in a century.

Early in April, most of the scaffolding had been removed from the new Opera House:

> people can realise the effect and proportions of this handsome addition to the leading buildings of the town. We are assured on the best authority that the Opera House will be second to none in the provinces.

In mid-April, the *Advertiser* appeared daily, to report the NUT conference held in the town, and then on 25 April, announcing that the theatre was rapidly approaching completion, gave a full description:

> Acting on the advice of their architect, Mr Frank Matcham, of London, the directors of the Gardens Company resolved to abandon all idea of altering their present Theatre, but to utilise this for a portion of a new scheme to be eventually carried out by him in improving the Gardens and the Pavilion buildings.
>
> The following is a full description of the Opera House as it will be when completed:-
>
> The old entrance and reading rooms have been removed, and on the site has been erected a handsome stone building with a frontage of about 73 feet to The Square, and a return front of 164 feet towards St John's Road.
>
> The side next to the Gardens is not much in evidence as the wall of the Theatre forms one side of the new glass and iron corridor to the Pavilion, which is approached from the grand entrance to the Gardens, the new facade is on an angle with the front of the Theatre, and is flanked by two dwarf stone towers with coloured glass domed roofs, and in the centre is the entrance containing the turnstiles and offices. A glass and iron shelter will protect the visitors on alighting from their carriages, and the whole forms a very imposing building, being designed in conjunction with the Theatre facade.

---

[4] Five atrocious cigarettes for one *old* penny. There were 240 old pennies in £1.
[5] 12½p, 17½p, 22½p.

The auditorium from the stage. The gasolier (centre of the oval panel in the ceiling) was restored and converted to natural gas in 1979 and now helps ventilation as it did in the Edwardian period.

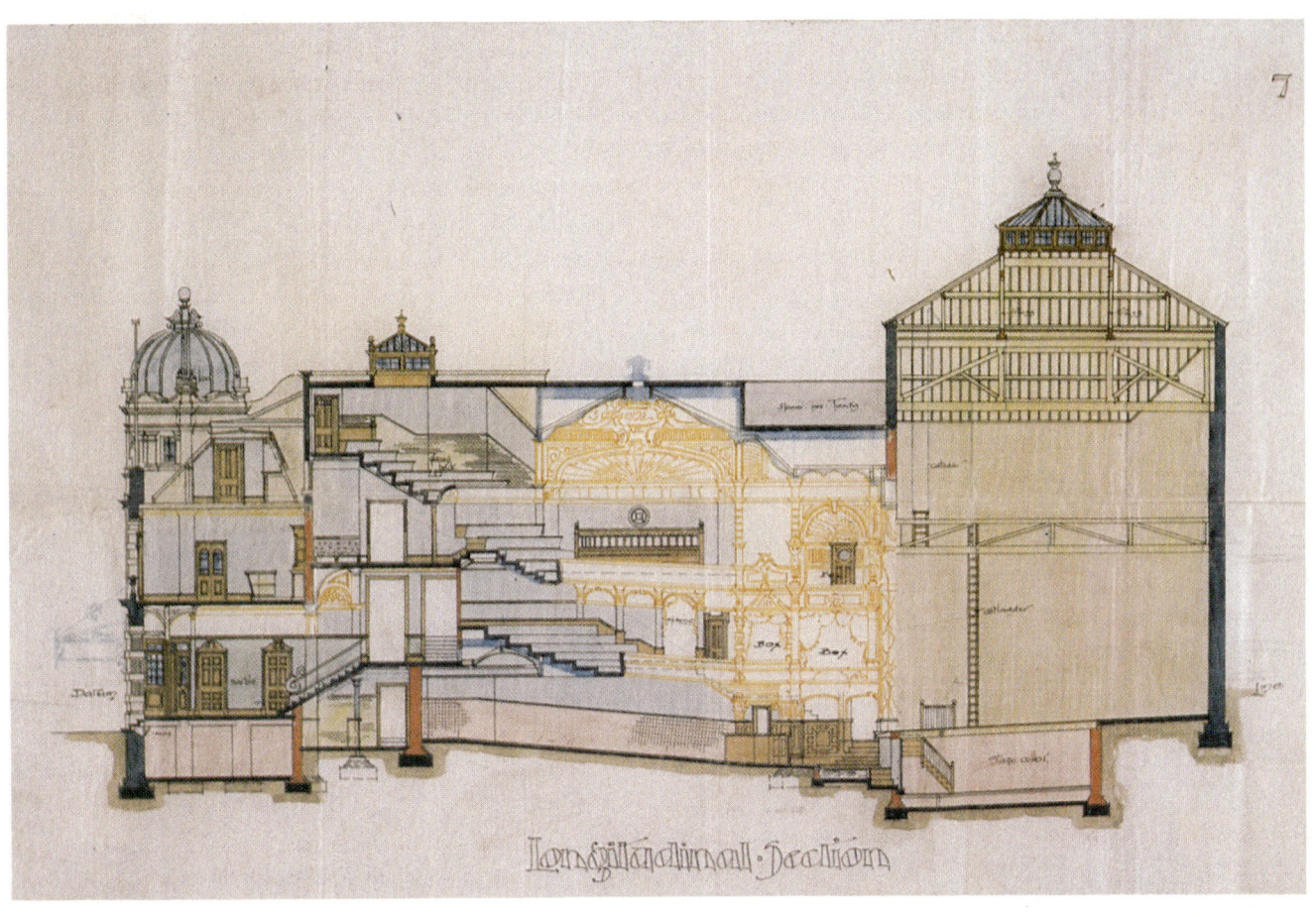

Longitudinal section: Buxton Opera House. One of a number of drawings by Frank Matcham now owned by High Peak Borough Council.

The Theatre is built on up to date lines, and with all the latest improvements, the floors, galleries, staircases and roof are all of concrete and iron, all passages and staircases are wide and commodious, and the exit doors are provided with Brigg's patent alarm exit bolts which prevent the doors being opened from the outside, but they give way to the slightest pressure from the inside.

A heavy fireproof curtain is provided to the stage opening, and the wall dividing the auditorium from the stage is continued up through the roof, iron doors prevent fire being carried up through the other openings. Hydrants fully equipped are provided in the most desirable positions, in fact, everything has been done for the safety of the public that human ingenuity and skill can suggest.

The sanitary and ventilation matters have had careful attention, there are retiring rooms fitted with every convenience for each class of the audience; large cloak rooms, smoke rooms, etc., have been provided and the comfort of the audience has had every consideration, this applies to the gallery and pit patrons equally to those in the stalls and dress circle.

The principal entrance is in the centre of the facade, here polished mahogany doors filled with brilliant glass will open into a very handsome vestibule where marble has been very extensively used, as on either side of the foot of the grand staircases which faces the entrance, are massive scrolls of polished alabaster supported on red marble bases, and at each side of these are white marble seats.

The grand staircase is constructed of white marble, the centre being covered with a rich Turkey carpet; this leads to the crush-room, the scheme of decoration from the vestibule being carried into this room except that the walls are panelled and filled in with silk tapestries.

On each side handsome draped openings lead into small lounges from which wide but short corridors conduct the visitors to the dress circle seats and the private boxes. Staircases at the end of these corridors are continued down to the stalls, which are furnished with thick carpet and four rows of luxurious tip-up arm seats; these are accessible, and are divided from the orchestra by a very handsome bold brass barrier draped with silk brocade.

The walls are covered with white Carrara marble, with plinths and bases of Emperors red marble.

The floors are inlaid Mosaic.

The ceiling is richly carved in raised plaster work, with a very fine artistic panel in the centre representing lyrical poetry, the side-panels being treated with musical trophies and flowers.

From the crush-room, small flights of steps lead into the rear seats of the dress circle.

This circle is fitted with comfortable striped velvet tip-up seats, and each seat obtains a clear and uninterrupted view of the stage and a fine view of the House.

Over the entrance vestibule is the grand foyer - a very handsome apartment; it is furnished with counter, etc., for dispensing refreshments. The floor is covered with Turkey carpets, and there are silk brocade draperies to the windows; the walls are covered with a leather paper, and the ceiling is richly decorated with raised ornamental cordelova. Mirrors and old prints adorn the walls, and luxurious lounges and settees help to furnish what will be a very delightful addition to the Theatre.

An improved attraction to the Theatre must not be overlooked, an entrance from the dress circle and stalls being obtained leading to the Gardens; this, especially in the summer, will form a most desirable lounge, and will no doubt be highly appreciated.

The pit is approached from St John's Road; here a shelter is provided, and the audience is conducted singly past the pay office to the wide promenade at the rear of the pit seats; these are provided with backs, and the whole covered with velvet; the floor is laid with inlaid linoleum and a particularly attractive feature is the tile covering of the walls, ensuring cleanliness and brightness in this part of the House.

A fine refreshment saloon is situated at the rear of the pit, well-lighted and ventilated and artistically decorated and furnished.

Retiring rooms for both sexes are provided in the most convenient and private positions.

The upper circle, which is over the dress circle, is approached by a wide fireproof staircase, from which the visitor is conducted through a fine crush-room into the centre of this circle and by corridors into side entrances; this will prevent crowding and easy access to the attractive velvet-covered seats. On each side of the upper circle is a large standing space with a curved handrail and balustrading, the whole forming an attractive feature to the Theatre.

The gallery is situated at the rear of the upper circle seats, but raised above same, giving the appearance of an additional tier; it is comfortably seated, and well ventilated, and provided with every requirement.

The auditorium is particularly well provided with exits, each part having in no case less than two, and these are so well designed that the building can be cleared in three minutes.

The decorations of the auditorium are carried out from Mr Matcham's designs, and are very rich; the style adopted is Louis XVI.

The ceiling is in the shape of an oval dome, formed into six painted panels representing music, painting, poetry, literature, dancing and comedy; a large curve shaped frieze joins this ceiling to the flat panelled ceiling over the stage, which contains paintings in monochrome, representing grace, strength and music.

The Buxton Coat-of-Arms, also treated in monochrome on a gold background, forms a graceful feature over the proscenium arch.

On each side of the proscenium are three private boxes, two on the dress circle level with light blue silk brocade and plush valences and curtains; these boxes are divided by beautiful columns of fine polished African onyx; a deep border of similar marble surrounds the stage opening, which has a deep valence corresponding with that to the boxes.

A feature is the top private boxes, caryatids support arches filled in with coved-shaped shells, and the effect is most artistic.

The fireproof curtain has been very artistically treated with a special design imitation iron grill, and the drop scene, by Hemsley, has been painted to accord with the general design of the Theatre.

The whole Theatre is brilliantly illuminated by the electric light, the fittings being specially designed to accord with the decorations, and which are light and very artistically treated.

The building throughout is heated by hot water pipes and radiators.

The stage is a large one, fitted up with flies, grid, and the usual working traps, bridges, etc, and includes the most recent and up to date improvements.

The dressing rooms are continued in a separate block of buildings, and are fitted up with every comfort, they are lighted by electricity and heated by hot water, and the artists interests have been well looked after by the architect.

It is intended to open the new House at Whitsuntide, and it is anticipated that the patronage of the inhabitants and visitors to Buxton will so far appreciate the new Theatre that its success will be assured.

This commendably detailed description omits one vital fact: colour. Fortunately, *The Builder* of 13 June 1903 records that the original palette was blue, gold and cream.[6] In a succinct paragraph, *The Builder* records all essential aspects, and remarks upon the entrance provided "direct from the Gardens to the dress circle and stalls" and to the "two refreshment saloons".

---

6 This information was much appreciated at the 1979 restoration.

Details of the Auditorium, Buxton Opera House.

Top left: The cherub on the right of the proscenium arch holds a real tambourine!

Lower left: Upper circle window. Mrs Nellie Wain, member of staff before 1920, remembers opening these windows, and others, every morning to air the theatre.

Above: Semi-circular tablet near the Exit (right) is adorned with the name Shakespeare. On the opposite side (not shown) is a similar tablet with the name Sullivan.

Part of the 1907-1911 programme cover which gives details of the interior long submerged: striped wall covering in the dress circle; two gangways in the pit; four rows of dress stalls divided from the orchestra by a curtained brass rail; padded bench seating in the pit (behind the stalls); heavily swathed curtains in the boxes; no projection room in the gallery; striped velvet seat covers in the dress circle and orchestra stalls; wide stairs in the foyer, covered with rich red Turkey carpet protected by white drugget renewed daily.

Twentieth century readers cannot fail to notice the tacit acceptance of social distinctions: retiring rooms fitted "with every convenience for each class of the audience" is worthy of note; so too the statement that every consideration had been given to the comfort of the audience: "this applies to the gallery and pit patrons equally to those in the stalls and dress circle". Equally? Rich carpets opposed to linoleum? Luxurious tip-up arm seats opposed to benches? Leather wall coverings and silk drapings, to wall tiles, no matter how hygienic?

The photograph on the cover of the 1907 programme shows us what an utterly charming interior awaited first-nighters on 1 June 1903. Before considering that sparkling occasion the *Advertiser* gave two further pieces of information on 30 May 1903. Under the headlines

> The New Opera House Licence
> Drinks Licence Refused
> Theatrical Licence Granted

the *Advertiser* reported what was to become an annual scenario for the next quarter of a century: Mr Willoughby and other directors requested a full licence for the theatre which would permit the sale of alcohol; the magistrates refused. Mr E. C. Milligan, Chairman of the Directors of the Gardens Company pointed out

> Ever since the old theatre was opened[7] we have always been told that we are so much behind the times, and that in no other part of the country would they have a theatre where refreshments are not to be had.

A Mr Batty, of Manchester, solicitor, said he appeared for a considerable list of people opposing the licence

> and represented most of the ministers of religion in Buxton - from the Unitarian to the Roman Catholic priest.
>
> The Chairman: I wish you could get them to agree in other matters.

Mr Batty declared he wished he could, and continued:

> To many subscribers, the main charm of the Buxton Gardens had been its peace and orderliness and quiet. The strongest, the unique attraction of the Gardens was its immunity from drink.

The argument wore on, but to no avail. And the refusal was reported in London. *The Era* of 30 May 1903 summed up thus:

> The majority of the townspeople and the directors of the Gardens Company, who are all men of prominent position in the town, never for a moment doubted the final issue. After a few moments' deliberation in private, the Bench pronounced their verdict. "We grant the dramatic licence on condition that you do not apply for excise". This undertaking, of course, had to be given. It is worthy of mention that the JPs adjudicating are members, with one exception, of the Union Club, which is at the very door of the Opera House.

The full licence was eventually granted early in January 1928. "Quarter of a Century late" was the *Advertiser* headline. Mr Batty's death was reported on 12 December 1926. And so it was over his dead body that the full licence was at last obtained.

In a special article by Edward Bradbury in May 1903, the *Advertiser* prepared the way for the First Night by giving information about the play to be performed at the opening of the Opera House: *Mrs Willoughby's Kiss,* a domestic drama in four acts "from the pen of Mr Frank Stayton, one of the youngest of English playwrights". It had been seen first at Brighton Theatre Royal on 2 May 1901 and in London at the Avenue Theatre on 18 October 1902. Dainty, pretty Mrs Willoughby and chattering, fidgetty Mrs Brandram are at the Grand Hotel, Plymouth, awaiting the return of their husbands from India. Brandram meets Mrs Willoughby and kisses her, thinking her the lovely wife he left fourteen years earlier to take up his duties in India. Discovery of his mistake causes embarrassment at first, but since Willoughby proves to be "a surly, stolid bear," Brandram and Mrs Willoughby admit their mutual attraction and plan to elope. Lilian Brandram persuades her father not to go. In the last act, Mrs Willoughby admits that she has decided not to leave her husband. "Now comes the didactic portion of the play", writes Mr Bradbury. Brandram is in

---
[7] In 1889.

OPERA HOUSE, BUXTON.

MONDAY, JUNE 1st, 1903, for Six Nights,
and SATURDAY MATINEE at 3.

Miss FLORENCE ST. JOHN and
Mr. SCOTT BUIST

with London Company,
Including Miss LILY HALL CAINE

Miss FLORENCE ST. JOHN.
Photo by Langfier.

"**Mrs. Willoughby's Kiss**"
Play in Four Acts, by FRANK STAYTON.

AND

"**My Milliner's Bill**"
By G. W. GODFREY.

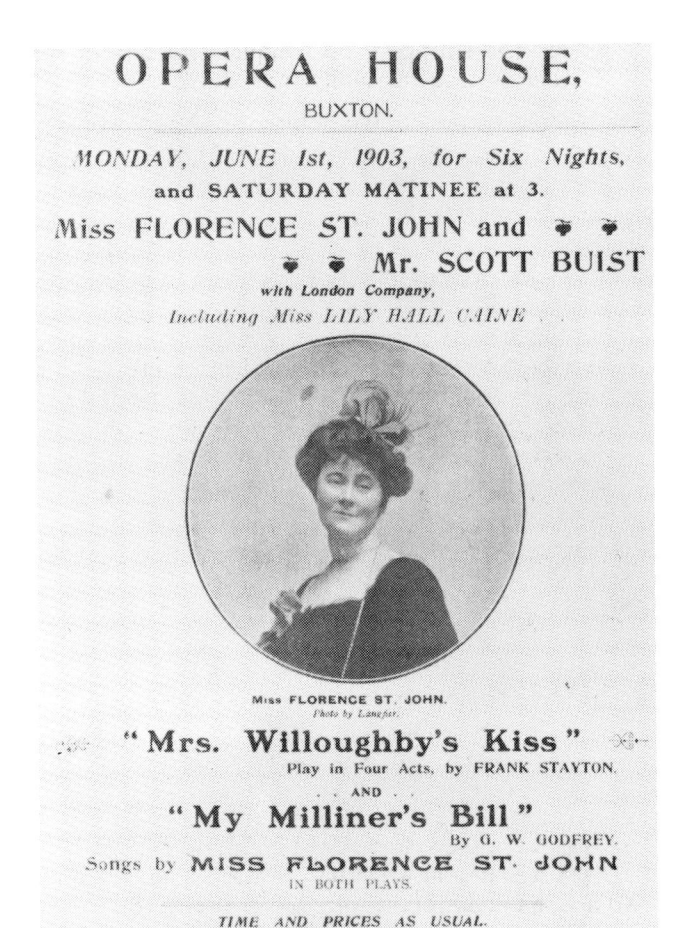

Songs by MISS FLORENCE ST. JOHN
IN BOTH PLAYS.

TIME AND PRICES AS USUAL.

Above: Playbill for the first play to be presented at Buxton Opera House.

Right: Details of entertainment in store for 1903 given on the back cover of the Opera House programme on June 1.

PROSPECTIVE ENGAGEMENTS: 1903.

May 31 (Sunday) at 8-15 p.m., Sacred Concert. Artistes: Mrs. Julian Clifford (Hon. Margaret Henniker), Miss Margaret Vereker, Mr. Anderson Nichol, Mr. Edwd. Cooper, and Mr. Julian Clifford.

June 1 (week) ... Miss Florence St. John, Miss Hall Caine, Mr. Scott Buist & Company in "Mrs. Willoughby's Kiss," and "My Milliner's Bill," from The Avenue Theatre, London. Miss Florence St. John will vary her songs in each piece nightly.

June 6 .... Grand Display of Fireworks and Illumination of Grounds by J. Pain & Sons, London.

June 9 and 10... "The Magistrate," by the Buxton Amateur Dramatic Society.

June 11, 12, 13... "Little Lord Fauntleroy."

June 18, 19, 20... "The Rose of the Riviera", new musical piece by F. Osmond Carr, composer of "In Town," "His Excellency," etc.

June 22 (week)... Mr. Tom Thorne and London Company in "Our Boys," "Confusion," and "The Guv'nor." Mr. Thorne will take his original parts.

June 29, 30 ...... "The Foundling," mus. farcical comedy
July 1 ....   from Terry's Theatre, London.

July 2, 3, 4 ...... "Somebody's Sweetheart," a musical comedy by Edward Morris.

July 4 .... The Hallé Choir Concert.

July 6, 7, 8 ...... "When We Were Twenty-One," from The Comedy Theatre, London.

July 9, 10, 11 ... "Why Smith Left Home" and "A Smart Set": Horace Lingard & Company from The Strand Theatre, London.

July 11 .... Grand Display of Fireworks and Illumination of Grounds by J. Pain & Sons, London.

July 13 (week)... D'Oyly Carte's Large Repertoire Company, in "The Mikado" "Yeomen of the Guard," "The Gondoliers," "Pinafore," etc.

July 20 (week)... Osmond Tearle Shakespearian Co.

July 27, 28, 29... Mr. and Mrs. Charles Sugden and Co.

July 30, 31, ... "There and Back," a musical comedy,
August 1 ....   from Shaftesbury Theatre, London.

Aug. 1 .... Grand Display of Fireworks and Illumination of Grounds by J. Pain & Sons, Loudon.

OTHER ARRANGEMENTS TO FOLLOW.

despair. His friend Lawrence Harvey points out:

> Suppose *you* had lost your good looks, while your wife retained hers. She would have put up with you.

Brandram "is thus brought to view the situation from another aspect" and "all ends happily" as the old story books say.

Ernest Bradbury hoped that *Mrs Willoughby's Kiss* would prove "a happy salute", and so it did. There were murmurings in the town, of course, intimating that the play had been chosen "on account of the name being identical with the cognomen of the genial General Manager and Secretary of the Pavilion Gardens Company".[8] Mr Bradbury pointed out the difficulties of selecting a really first class London company for the opening of a new theatre. Dates have to be arranged far in advance. "Perhaps at Whitsuntide" would not be acceptable as the basis of booking a touring company. Mr Willoughby had done well to make such an attractive booking in the midst of building operations.

A Notable Triumph

Under those words, the *Buxton Advertiser* gave an eager town details of the opening "to public view" of the new Opera House on Saturday 30 May 1903. "Favoured with delightful weather", the Directors of the Buxton Gardens Company gave a luncheon at the George Hotel for members of the Press. Mr E. C. Milligan, chairman, welcomed the guests who included Mr Frank Matcham, architect, and declared his belief that the new theatre would

> conduce very much to the enjoyment of the visitors who came there, and place Buxton in the highest ranks of watering-places.

Having drunk to the success of the new theatre, the company adjourned to the building

> where a first-class programme of instrumental music was performed under the direction of Mr De Jong and greatly enjoyed.

Later, members of the public were admitted, free, and soon the house was full:

> Everybody present expressed themselves charmed with this latest addition to the resources of the Buxton Gardens Company.

Two days later, on Monday 1 June 1903, many of them were again at the Opera House, to witness the first performance of the first play presented there. The *Buxton Advertiser* waxed almost lyrical in honour of the occasion:

> Whilst recollecting the opening of the Buxton Pavilion and Gardens in August 1871, and the opening of the Concert Hall in 1876, in both of which ceremonies the late Duke of Devonshire took a leading part; we confidently assert that nothing ever gave greater pleasure to a larger number of people in Buxton than the opening of the new Opera House on Monday night.

> By seven o'clock there was a great crowd round the entrance, and when the doors were opened the unallotted portions of the theatre were filled immediately without any apparent abatement of the crush. Shortly after seven-thirty carriages began to roll up, and the stalls and dress circle were soon filled with an assemblage which, we were glad to see, was very representative of Buxton.

> A few minutes after eight, at a signal from the musical conductor, Mr Herman Kiel, the whole house rose while the National Anthem was played. It was a grand spectacle, the beautiful dresses and coiffures of the ladies putting the finishing touch to the chaste elegance and softened light of the beautiful building. Then the drop-scene was raised and Miss Evelyn Aylestone appeared.

She spoke *The Prologue,* a fine piece of Edwardian sententiousness, written for the occasion by two local gentlemen: Mr A. G. Sparrow of Green Fairfield and Mr A. P. Shaw of Whitehall:

> A greeting, friends, I bring to one and all
> Who dwell within this land of lonely dales,

---

[8] The matter does not appear to have been considered important in the Willoughby family. Miss Margery Willoughby, born 1905, daughter of Arthur, never heard any reference to it, but remarked: "I don't think my grandmother would have been pleased."

This town of grey, set high amid the hills,
Fronting the open moorland and the streams
That silver-footed dance unto the plains
'Mid wealth of daffodil, and country cheer.
From out my heart a two-fold greeting speaks
To you, who, for a little in our midst,
Seek out the crown of health, the upland air,
The bright enchantment of a holiday;
When home shall once more claim you, may the
                                            thought
Of us, and ours, be pleasant memories.
In chief, to-night, I bid all welcome here,
Within the precincts of this tree-girt shrine,
Set in the fairest garden of the land;
Here Art and Craftsmanship have reared a home
Worthy our English stage, the mimic rites
Thalia taught the Greeks when earth was young.
So may the gods that in the gallery dwell,
Gaze down upon the goddesses who haunt
The stalls, the golden circle, and the pit,
And all may look with wonder on a stage
Where Love and Hate, Vice, Virtue, Sorrow, Joy,
Through human lips, cry out, HUMANITY.

But come, my muse, and tread a merrier measure.
Here in the hub of Buxton's wheel of pleasure,
Here in our Gardens, where to please the sight,
Bower and lawn, and waterfall unite.
We view once more the well-remembered scene:
The sober veterans, bowling on the green;
The youth and maiden, in an under-tone,
Murm'ring beside the drowsy chaperone,
Who, 'mid the strains of music idly napping,
Hears in her dreams, the croquet mallets tapping;
Some, on the tennis-court, pursue the ball,
Int'rested only in the score "love all";
While others, if the day be warm and sunny,
Drift round the lake and into matrimony;
Here invalids are on the terrace sitting,
And children are at play, and nurses knitting;
While the bath-chairman audibly enlarges
On Buxton's beauties to his gouty charges.
But stay my muse, here's surely something new,
What pile is this that breaks upon the view!

Pillar and cornice doth its front adorn.
And sporting cherub sports a tandem horn.
Why, it's an Opera House! Oh, Buxton, you've
                                            meant
For many years to make this great improvement
Now, as you gaze upon this fair outside,
At length completed, say with proper pride,
"These things are good, above, below, around,
The like to MATCH'EM surely can't be found!"
And, as without, so too, within we see
How Art and Craft unite in harmony;
How form and colour, tastefully combined,
Attract the eye, and stimulate the mind.
And I am here to ask - what you can guess -
Your kindly aid to make it a success.
Help out our efforts for your delectation.
Don't let us suffer undeserved stagnation.
With your support, we stand; without it, fail.
That is the moral that adorns the tale.

And now, farewell; not with sad heart, as one
Who fain would linger by the side of love;
But with glad eyes, for we to-night shall lift
The garden-latch that leads to Fairyland.

These, the first words uttered on the stage of Buxton Opera House, were, the *Advertiser* tells us,

admirably chosen and very nicely spoken.

Miss Aylestone was heartily applauded and presented with a beautiful bouquet. Then the play began "and ran merrily from start to finish." *Mrs Willoughby's Kiss,* a domestic drama in four acts by Mr Frank Stayton, was cast as follows:

"MRS WILLOUGHBY'S KISS!"

Oswald Brandram	Mr Scott-Buist
Lawrence Harvey	Mr James Lindsay
Rupert Willoughby	Mr Horton Cooper
Frank Dale	Mr Athol Stewart
Robert	Mr J. G. Taylor, junior
Lilian Brandram	Miss Florence Jackson
Clacher	Miss Nancy Clive
Mrs Willoughby	Miss Lily Hall Caine
Mrs Brandram	Miss Florence St John

Miss Florence St John, "inimitable" as Mrs Brandram, kept the house in roars of laughter, but showed "a beautiful bit of pathos" as the curtain fell; Miss Lily Hall Caine "established herself a great favourite" as Mrs Willoughby, and came well out of "a difficult part"; Miss Florence Jackson was "very loving and tender"; Mr Scott-Buist "was on the full stretch all the time". Mr James Lindsay "did much to make the play run smoothly" and Mr Frank Dale did his part of the play "mostly spooning" as if to the manner born. "Altogether it was a good combination and an excellent impersonation". Lovely bouquets were handed to the ladies at the close of the play, when there were loud calls for Mr John Willoughby. He was "very warmly welcomed" when he came on stage to say

> Ladies and Gentlemen, - I wish I was in the happy position of being able to invite you to "charge your glasses and drink success to the New Opera House." (Loud applause.) We have now, I am pleased to say, a theatre which affords accommodation to the largest touring companies, but this beautiful house cannot be maintained unless we receive the patronage of the residents of this town, and I think my directors may reasonably expect that patronage from you. (Applause.) I have, in their name, to offer you a very excellent list of engagements this year, and I can, without hesitation, assure you that if you support this house as I hope you will, the list of engagements will improve year by year and become still more attractive. (Applause.) I have in the name of my directors to welcome you heartily, and thank you for your presence. I am quite sure you are delighted with the appearance of this House internally and externally, and there is one gentleman present who is very proud of his handiwork. With your permission I will call upon Mr Matcham. (Loud applause.)[9]

Mr Matcham, "flatteringly received", walked to the front of the curtain. He said:

> Ladies and Gentlemen, - I am sure it is very kind indeed to ask me to come before you to receive your kind congratulations. It is very kind of Mr Willoughby to make the very flattering remarks he has made. But you don't want a long speech from me, so if you will allow me to retire I will do by expressing the heartiest wish for the success of the new Buxton Theatre. (Applause.)[10]

The *Buxton Advertiser* concluded the report of this sparkling occasion with special commendation of the Opera House Orchestra which "created a very favourable impression" under the direction of Mr Kiel. The orchestra had been engaged for the season:

> To have a permanent Orchestra as well as a new Opera House will be much appreciated by theatregoers.

The Era of 6 June 1903 tells us that after Mr Matcham's thanks to the audience "for the compliment they had paid him", the farce *My Milliner's Bill* was played. Miss St John and Mr Scott-Buist "created roars of laughter" and Miss St John's singing of *Sally in our Alley* was loudly encored. *The Era* report concludes with a graceful tribute to Mr Arthur Willoughby, the acting-manager, who worked so hard for everybody's comfort, and records that the contractors were Messrs Vickers and Sons of Nottingham, suppliers of chairs for the theatre were Lyons and Co, scenery was by Hemsley and decorations by F. de Jong and Co.

Buxton was delighted. The dear old *Advertiser* determined to leave no point unstressed, began its editorial on 3 June 1903:

> By building such a lovely place, the Directors of the Buxton Gardens Company have shown that, at last, they have learned the lesson that they must spend one sovereign to earn two, and if they persevere in this enlightened policy, they will find that the Theatre itself will pay its own way without the adventitious aids of advertisements on programmes and poor penny-in-the-slot royalties - which two forms of revenue savour more of tripperdom than stately Buxton.

---

[9] The Buxton Advertiser and List of Guests, 6 June 1903.
[10] Ibid.

The writer asked Buxtonian theatre goers to decide which was easier: to support a lovely theatre at their own door, or to travel to a grimy city (Manchester) to spend three hours in a theatre, only to reach home after midnight, "refreshed" by long hours spent on the railway and in "sundry cabs"....

For much of the next two decades, the Opera House was a tolerably successful touring theatre. Companies came, week by week, bringing a variety of entertainment: comedy, tragedy, melodrama, farce, burlesque, musical comedy, revue, opera, ballet. In the course of a year every type of theatre-going brow, high, middle and low, had something to please. "Get the OHH - Opera House Habit"[11] urges a programme note in November 1928.

Before the end of the first year, several famous actor-managers had sent companies to Buxton, and many became regular visitors over the years. A brief notice in *The Era* in mid-August 1903 recorded the ultimate theatrical accolade:

> SIR HENRY IRVING, who was present last Thursday evening at a performance of *Monsieur Beaucaire*, at the New Opera House, Buxton, told Mr Arthur Willoughby he - Sir Henry - was delighted with the beautiful theatre, and complimented Mr Oswald Brookes, the manager for Mr Wilfred Cotton, on the excellence of the company. Sir Henry Irving on Monday witnessed the performance of Mr H. Beerbohm Tree's company in *The Eternal City*.

To have the approval of Sir Henry Irving, the foremost Victorian actor manager and the first actor to be knighted, was approval indeed.

Shakespeare companies abounded in the Edwardian years and after: Mr F. R. Benson,[12] Osmond Tearle, Ian Maclaren, Allan Wilkie, Alexander Marsh, Florence Glossop-Harris and Frank Cellier, Lena Ashwell, Henry Baynton, Charles Doran and others brought their companies here. The repertoire tended to be "Merry Shrews of Venice"[13] and artistic standards were not always high, but Buxton school children were fortunate to have opportunities to meet Shakespeare first 'on the boards' instead of on the page as most children alas! do now.

Opera companies were almost as numerous as Shakespearean, some of them with imposing names: the Cavaliere F. Castellano English and Italian Grand Opera Company, the Empire Grand Opera Company, the Harrison Frewin Opera Company, the E. St Alban's Opera Company, are examples. Again, their repertoire was 'safe' and strictly limited. The Carl Rosa, Sadler's Wells, D'Oyly Carte and others ensured that Buxtonians became familiar with some, at least, of the repertoire: *Faust, Il Trovatore, 'Cav and Pag', Rigoletto, Carmen, Madame Butterfly* and *Maritana* were the most popular. The Castellano Company in July 1914 anticipated the 1979 Festival by presenting Donizetti's *Bride of Lammermoor*.

Theatre programmes are rich hunting grounds for stage historians. Familiar names lurk in almost every cast list. Buxton's programmes are no exception. Even a cursory glance through some of the bound copies in the Library produce treasures which may then be followed up by reading the reviews in the ever faithful *Buxton Advertiser and List of Guests*. Miss Italia Conti, dancing teacher to Royalty, played here in two Henry Arthur Jones plays in 1903, Mrs Patrick Campbell "and her entire London company" gave a special "Flying Matinee"[14] performance of Pinero's *The Second Mrs Tanqueray* in November 1903, Mr Marvin Harvey made the first of numerous visits in 1904, Ben Greet and Company, Edward Compton (father of Sir Compton Mackenzie the

---

[11] a habit still to be recommended.

[12] Later Sir Frank Benson, Knighted by King George V in 1916 in the interval of a performance at the Shakespeare Tercentenary Celebrations at the Theatre Royal, Drury Lane.

[13] A neat title invented by J. C. Trewin, drama critic of *The Illustrated London News*, and author of numerous books on theatrical subjects. In ten Shakespeare seasons between 1903 and 1920 at Buxton, *Merchant of Venice* was offered in all ten, *Hamlet* in nine, *Taming of the Shrew* in eight, *Twelfth Night* in seven, *Merry Wives of Windsor* in six.

[14] Railways were then so well organised that London companies could give an early matinee performance at a provincial theatre and return to London in time for their evening performance.

in Shaw's *Candida* in 1909. Gertrude Lawrence played Blanche Marie in *The Little Michus,* billed as the greatest French Military Musical Comedy success ever produced by Mr George Edwards. Evelyn Laye and Dodie Smith were in the cast of *Mr Wu* in 1916; *It's a Bargain,* in 1917 and 1918, had Archie Pitt and Gracie Fields in the cast, as well as "the Star Sextette of Dancers and some Bonnie Girls"! Robertson Hare played in *Oh! Alexander* and *The Muddler* in 1919, Hermione Gingold played Dolly in Bernard Shaw's *You Never Can Tell* in April 1920. A high spot in October 1925 was the performance by Anna Pavlova[15] and her London company, watched from a box by Douglas Fairbanks senior and Mary Pickford. Quotation from the *Advertiser* review of that memorable occasion is obligatory: it seems that the house was full to overflowing; the great dancer performed within a simple setting, a light blue curtain as background; her programme included Chopiniana, Valse Caprice and The Swan. In intense silence, she danced

> seeming to float through space, pausing a moment and then taking on fresh life - but ever seeming to have come but for the moment, something intangible which might fade away at the slightest sound...

Superb, the *Advertiser* critic decided, was the only word to describe her. Other names to excite us from these early years are Robert Newton, Felix Aylmer, Barry Jackson, John Drinkwater, Esmé Percy, W. Bridges-Adams (later Director of the Memorial Theatre, Stratford upon Avon), the Birmingham Repertory Company, the Abbey Players, Dublin.

The Opera House has staged ballet, boxing revues, musical comedies, vaudeville and the circus! The Great War period was particularly rich in revues, musicals and burlesques. Some of the programmes make amusing reading:

> the Curios, seven brilliant stars in a Wedgwood

Douglas Fairbanks senior and Mary Pickford outside the Palace Hotel, Buxton, during their visit to Derbyshire in 1924 to prepare the film Dorothy Vernon of Haddon Hall in which Miss Pickford played Dorothy Vernon.

writer, and of Miss Fay Compton) came with his celebrated Compton Comedy Company; Gordon Harker was 2nd gentleman in *Othello* in May 1907, Basil Dean played small 'character' parts in July 1907, and appeared

[15] Anna Pavlova 1882-1931, famous and much loved ballerina. Trained in the strict Russian Imperial School, she came to Europe with Diaghilev's Ballets Russes in 1909 and 1910, but later toured the world with her own company. She included some English dancers, an unusual occurrence in that period, and hence deserves honour as a benefactor of English ballet.

setting; the Sequins, bright, brisk and breezy; Fred Karno's enormous success *Mumming Birds;* the Chocs, a pleasing packet of Piquant and Palatable Performers; the Follies - this programme is subject to alteration and repairs; Charles Heslop's Brownies - no expense has been spared... the Expense, like all the rest, is simply awful... *She Slipped* - gorgeous Musical Farcical Comedy, screamingly funny from start to finish.

If the Opera House management of these early decades had heeded the *Advertiser* strictures concerning such "adventitious aids" to revenue as advertisements on programmes, we should have lost much charming amusement and some fascinating glimpses of life in Buxton in times before our own. Half an hour on a rainy day spent browsing through the Library collection of early programmes will always reveal treasures. Particularly entertaining are management requests and suggestions: Ladies, for example, are asked

> not to stick hat pins in the back of the seat in front. The practice is both dangerous and destructive.

What was a poor lady to do, observing, as she must, the peremptory

> No hats or bonnets allowed in the Stalls or First Three Rows of the Dress Circle?

She could take comfort from the announcement that the Opera House, Buxton, is

> The Safest and Most Beautiful Theatre in the Kingdom

whilst pondering her reply to the stark question

> Do you Roller Skate?

In the dark days of 1914, it must have been some consolation to read on every programme:

> The Opera House will be open each week during the coming Autumn and Winter. Warm and comfy. Popular prices.

As the dreadful war dragged on, other notices were included:

> NCOs and Privates Half Price (Stalls, Family Circle, Pit Stalls and Pit) except Saturday evening.
> Military Notice - Tickets for all parts may be purchased at the Gardens Entrance, and on producing same, late pass obtained

Anna Pavlova (1882-1931) in her famous "Swan" costume. Douglas Fairbanks and Mary Pickford returned to Buxton to watch her performance in 1925.

Repeatedly, companies felt obliged to include the information, as time went on:

> All the Gentlemen of the Company are either Ineligible for Military Service or have been Discharged after serving with the Colours.

When some particularly big attraction was billed, patrons would read

> Free List entirely suspended

a reminder of the custom, still observed, of "papering"

the house,[16] particularly at the beginning of a week. Nothing succeeds like success! People developing the habit of smoking "atrocious cigarettes" were the subject, repeatedly, of disapproving letters in the *Advertiser,* and had to read their programme carefully, since rules changed somewhat capriciously:

> No Smoking during this engagement

could be followed the next week by

> Smoking permitted evenings only.

Visits by Martin Harvey and Company always occasioned a ban on smoking. This must have seemed ironical because, repeatedly, the Company included *A Cigarette Makers Romance* in the week's repertoire.

Charley's Aunt by Brandon Thomas was first presented at the Opera House in 1904, with the information

> From Brazil, where the nuts come from.

Apparently it was then nearing its "one hundred thousandth performance". There would be many more performances of it in Buxton in years to come.

Who could resist

> An Extraordinary Play. The King and Queen, The Prince and Princess of Wales have all witnessed this play, the Princess having seen it twice?[17]

The play was Jerome K. Jerome's *The Passing of the Third Floor Back,* first seen in Buxton in 1910. In 1911, November's "Extra Special Attraction" was *Uncle Tom's Cabin* with Real Negroes. Full Chorus!

A year later a programme announces:

> J. Pitt-Hardacre and Co. of London Artistes who appeared before HRH the Duchess of Fife... in the Great Pathetic Play...
>
> East Lynne
>
> The Soul-Stirring Production, the most successful ever written, is now approaching its 14,000th Night, and is in a Prologue (written expressly for this tour by J. Pitt-Hardacre) and Four Acts, depicting
>
> The Murder, The Elopement, A Life Ruined, The Atonement for Sin Committed, The Husband's Forgiveness.
>
> The only Recognised Version, and the only one containing the Comic Policeman, Bullock.
> (NB. Prologue: The Cause of it All)

When George Bernard Shaw's play *Pygmalion,* first seen in London in 1914, came to Buxton in 1915, Opera House patrons were given a passage from Nash's Magazine to arouse their interest:

> No recent play has evoked so much discussion or enjoyed so huge a success as Mr Bernard Shaw's *Pygmalion.* Its sheer audacity won for it a vogue quite unprecedented in the annals of modern social satire; it has been the regret of thousands that they have not had the opportunity of actually viewing its unfolding upon the stage[18]

The play was again seen at the Opera House in 1917.

The Great War, 1914-18, in which so many brave lives were lost, brought changes to the Opera House. The stately, week by week procession of London companies, bringing West End successes, plays in the classical repertory and revivals, with regular "doses" of opera, ballet and musical comedy, weakened and eventually almost perished. Audiences changed too. The spacious days when carriages rolled up around 7.30pm and Nellie Wain and her colleagues showed fashionably attired people to the Dress Stalls, each seat with a freshly laundered antimacassar on the back, were going. Soon, servicemen brandishing tickets which compelled their NCOs to give a late pass were frequenting the theatre, and a seemingly endless number of revues and variety shows were presented, three local men providing such

---

[16] Giving free seats ie complimentary tickets.
[17] Edward VII and Queen Alexandra. The Prince and Princess of Wales became King George V and Queen Mary after King Edward's death in 1910.
[18] Mrs Patrick Campbell was the first Eliza Doolittle when *Pygmalion* was first presented in 1914. When a film version was shown at the Odeon in Chesterfield in the 1930s, with Wendy Hiller as Eliza, 21,000 seats were sold in a week. Chesterfield's population then was 23,000.

entertainment when professional sources failed. There was a growing interest in films - silent at first - and old programmes reveal that the illustrated lecture, particularly if illustrated by moving pictures, could be seen at the Opera House. *Kinemacolour,* in an up-to-date entertainment with vocalists, here in 1913 and 1914, showed such items as Carnival at Nice, Studies in Natural Colours, Ice Skating at Murren, British Soldiers, Church Parade at Aldershot, Presentation of Colours at Sandhurst. Rivetting! And, of course, "as given before TM the King and Queen and Members of the Royal Family." Arthur B. Malden's Cinematograph Travel Talks included (1915) Brave Little Belgium, Paris, Our Empire. August 1916 brought The Great Spectacle

BRITAIN PREPARED
A grand Kinematograph revue of the activities of
His Majesty's Naval and Military Forces.
Daily at 11.30, 3 and 8pm
Saturday matinee 2.45pm

In October 1916 D. W. Griffith's "mighty spectacle" *The Birth of a Nation* was shown twice daily, 2.45 and 8pm. This great film, still respected, was billed almost as a sheet of statistics:

18000 people
5000 horses
3000 scenes
8 months to perfect
Cost £100,000

but viewers were assured:

> The Birth of a Nation will never be presented in anything but the highest class Theatres, and at prices charged for the best Theatrical Attractions.

Amazingly, after the war, the theatrical profession quickly revived: the Opera House was again open almost every week of the year and the old touring round appeared to have returned. But wars have dreadful aftermaths. In June 1921, the *Advertiser* reported

A FILM WEEK
Mr Hastings[19] was unable, owing to the present difficulties in the theatrical world, to book a suitable

Buxton Opera House staff, 1932, photographed when the theatre was wired for talking films. Back row, from left: Pageboy Bernard Duffley, cashier Florence Turner (now Mrs Smith), cashier Maud Harris (now Mrs Lindop), usherette Millie King (now Mrs Winterbotham), commissionaire George Baker, usherette Hilda Chambers, usherette Beatrice Bates and trainee projectionist Bill Bromley. Front row, from left: Projectionists Bobby Quinney and Harold Pritchard, manager "Tiny" Richardson, head cashier Mary Hargreaves and supervisor Florence Starkey.

company for this week, and had to fall back on a film...

The film was *Kismet,* "the Greatest of all Pictures", "The Romance and Gorgeous Splendour of the East."

1921 was a disastrous year. The *Advertiser* provides much gloomy reading, particularly with regard to the great miners' strike. The editorial of 2 July 1921 begins to sound a more hopeful note, reminding readers that with the coal strike now over, the cotton trade dispute settled, engineers ready to accept the terms offered and the olive branch held out to Ireland, the time has come to make up the losses of the past disastrous months. Two weeks later,

---

[19] Mr F. A. Hastings was manager of the Opera House 1912 to 1926, with a short break for war service.

under an editorial headed Sunny Buxton, the most frequently overheard remark in the town is quoted: "The finest summer we have known".[20] This sustained period of brilliant sunshine and intense heat was not, alas, an augury of economic bliss ahead. The Buxton Gardens Company had not paid dividends for some years, there were more and more weeks when Mr Hastings booked films for the Opera House, more "spectaculars" at first, including D. W. Griffith's *Intolerance,* but eventually such less demanding material as *Alf's Button,* billed as

The Picture that made the Prince of Wales laugh.

In 1927 Buxton Corporation acquired the Pavilion Gardens and all the properties formerly owned by the Gardens Company. The Opera House was closed for a week in January 1928 for reseating. It was at this time, presumably that the pit benches, behind the four rows of Dress Stalls, were removed, and red plush tip-up seats were provided in what were now called pit stalls, either side of a centre gangway. The photographs of the auditorium on programme covers from 1907 show two gangways in the pit benches, but the 1928 reseating removed these, and the 1979 restoration kept the 1928 single centre gangway in the Stalls. The old arrangement of four rows of Dress Stalls, separated from the orchestra by a handsome, curtained brass rail, with rows of Pit benches beyond, reaching to the rear of the auditorium area, was thus destroyed in 1928. The whole seating area below stage level and beyond the orchestra pit was henceforth known as the Stalls. Since 1979 Stalls are usually designated Front, Middle and Rear, and vary in price, Front Stalls usually being the most expensive.

There were unsettled years, inevitably, after the change of ownership of the Opera House. Some brave touring companies still came, but by 1913 there were rumblings:

back again to concert parties twice nightly..

was the comment in January that year. By May, Major H. C. Lings wrote to the *Advertiser,* deploring the poor audiences at the Opera House: the usual support, he claimed, ran to a round dozen or so in the Stalls, two attenuated rows in the Dress Circle and, at most, a half-filled Pit area and Upper Circle. Meanwhile, there were warm debates in the council chamber about the expenses of running the Gardens, and two interesting suggestions in the *Advertiser* soon to be acted upon: wire the Opera House for Talkies and emulate the success of Malvern and have a Drama Festival at the Opera House. The suggestion of Talkies evokes strong protest; musicians would be out of work. To keep silent films would help to keep down unemployment. But nothing could stop the mighty film juggernaut. Within a very short time, the Opera House was duly "wired", sound equipment was installed and from 1932 a long, long period as a cinema began. The Festival suggestion required a longer gestation period, but by 1937 that too became reality, and Buxton Opera House once again filled columns in the national press.

[20] 1921 was the year when the Borough Council put a curb on loquacious members by limiting speeches to five minutes.

CHAPTER SIX

Festivals

"WHAT about it, Buxton?"

R. J. Finnemore asked the question at the end of an article in the Daily Despatch on 31 July 1936. He had just returned from a visit to the Malvern Festival in Worcestershire, and confessed to feeling pangs of jealousy:

> Everything proclaimed theatre: the streets gay with bunting, the crowds flocking to the box office, the packed hotels, and the patronal figure of Shaw[1] himself in Norfolk suit, followed everywhere by venerating glances.

The Malvern Festival had been started eight years previously, thanks to the inspiration of Sir Barry Jackson,[2] founder and director of the Birmingham Repertory Company, working in association with Malvern Repertory Theatre. Sir Barry explained the birth of the Festival as

> A desire to bring together some of those having a sincere interest in the theatre for a few days in place of the customary few hours.... Such a scheme necessitated a locality with just sufficient communal life to form a centre, yet lacking the so-called amenities which make existence in a modern city almost unbearable.

Mr Finnemore felt that it was time for the North to have a Theatre Festival. He suggested Buxton as the ideal location, and named Mr William Armstrong[3] of the Liverpool Playhouse as a theatre genius capable of organising a festival which would, in time, rival Malvern's.

> Money must be found at the outset for such a venture. As Buxton would benefit financially from any plan calculated to attract visitors from all over the world for a solid month, I hope that the Buxton Corporation will send a representative to Malvern.

PAVILION GARDENS & OPERA HOUSE
Home of the Buxton Theatre Festival

Cover of the Old Vic Theatre Festival programme, Buxton Opera House, 1937. The original, in colour, cost two old pence. The illustration captures the festive atmosphere the Old Vic Company brought to Buxton. The tree on the left in the forecourt is still sadly missed by elderly Buxtonians.

---

[1] George Bernard Shaw, 1856-1950, dramatist and critic.
[2] Sir Barry Jackson, 1879-1961. Director, manager and dramatist. Founded the Malvern Festival 1929. Director of the Memorial Theatre, Stratford-on-Avon 1945-48. Knighted 1925.
[3] William Armstrong. Director and producer of Liverpool Playhouse 1922-41.

One of the famous Bernard Shaw post cards. GBS conducted a massive correspondence throughout his life, much of it on postcards. Extant examples are now prized by collectors. Fortunately Mr J Boddington, manager of the Pavilion Gardens, ignored Mr Shaw's strictures, and invited Lilian Baylis to provide festival productions for Buxton.

Their next move should be to approach the Opera House management.

As we know, the idea of a Theatre Festival at the Opera House had already been mooted in 1930. Imagine the delight of seeing it in print in a national daily, and with such august names attached! Even whilst Bernard Shaw was penning one of his famous postcards in response to R. J. Finnemore's article, Mr J. E. Boddington, manager of the Pavilion Gardens, sprang into action. His passionate persuasion in the Council Chamber finally triumphed, but only thanks to the Mayor's casting vote in favour.

Mr Finnemore had hinted at the desirability of the Shavian presence, should a Buxton Festival materialise. He reminded readers of Mr Shaw's holiday in the town some years previously. Buxton remembered; Mr Shaw had suggested nationalising the banks! To Mr Finnemore GBS wrote

> As I have a direct commercial interest in theatrical festivals, my approval of them is of no value. They must, however, be locally managed. It is silly to ask Sir Barry Jackson or Mr William Armstrong, whose hands are already more than full, to go to Buxton. They can only invite Buxton in reply to go to Blazes. If Buxton cannot organise its own cultural activities it must do without them.

Buxton did not go to Blazes, but to the Old Vic.[4] Miss Lilian Baylis,[5] manager, agreed to bring the Old Vic

---

[4] Old Vic: built in the Waterloo Road, south of the River Thames, in 1818 as the Royal Coburg Theatre, later renamed the Victoria Theatre. Emma Cons took it over in 1880 as a temperance hall: the Royal Victoria Hall and Coffee Tavern. Lady Frederick Cavendish gave her considerable help, financial and social.

[5] Lilian Baylis 1874-1937. Founder-manager of the Old Vic and Sadlers Wells companies. From 1898 she helped her aunt Emma Cons at the "Vic", taking over management in 1914. She provided opera and good drama for the masses ("my people.") Between 1914 and 1923 all Shakespeare's plays had been presented at the Old Vic as the theatre came to be known. Sadlers Wells opened in 1931 and became the home of opera and ballet. The Ninth Duke of Devonshire had given money to help Miss Baylis to acquire this theatre. She was appointed Companion of Honour in 1929. She shared with Queen Mary the distinction of an Honorary MA from the University of Oxford and wore her cap, gown and hood on first nights and other "occasions." Long before the National Theatre was built, people thought of the Old Vic as our National Theatre, a view encouraged and endorsed by Miss Baylis.

Company to Buxton in August and September 1937, prior to the opening of the Old Vic autumn season. The Company would normally be in rehearsal some of that time, preparing for their next season.

The Buxton Festival dates were agreed: 30 August to 18 September. Three plays would be presented and in such a way that it would be possible to see all three in one week. Ivor Brown congratulated Buxton in the Observer of 15 August 1937:

> The Derbyshire Festival will be a prelude to the activities of the Old Vic Company. That is now the only way in which a brief Festival can be financed; it must be the appendage of a season elsewhere. It is very sensible of Buxton to remember its theatre as well as its golf courses, tennis courts and croquet lawns. It shows surprising lack of enterprise that more cities have not realised the opportunities of a dramatic Festival.

Miss Lilian Baylis saw *all* the possibilities:

> We love the place, the air is a tonic, and if audiences are as the scenery there can be no doubt about the success of the Festival

She carefully added the words

> Local staff cheque payable to Lilian Baylis every Friday[6]

to the draft letter outlining the financial arrangements made for the Theatre Festival.

Three plays were announced: Bernard Shaw's *Pygmalion*. Ibsen's *Ghosts* and Shakespeare's *Measure for Measure*. Members of the company included Diana Wynyard, Robert Morley, Mark Dignam, Stephen Murray, Jay Laurier, Marie Ney, Emlyn Williams, Jean Cadell and Sylvia Coleridge.

The Vicar of Buxton ensured the success of the Festival by condemning *Ghosts*[7] and *Measure for Measure*. He

Lilian Baylis CH, MA Oxon(Hon), LLD Birm(Hon) 1874-1937.

---

[6] The original may be seen at Buxton Art Gallery and Museum.

[7] When Ibsen's *Ghosts* was presented at the Opera House in 1917 it was billed as "The Family Tragedy."

objected to what he considered the "loose morals" characteristic of both plays:

> Surely it would have been simple to select plays which were wholesome and calculated to improve the general moral tone.[8]

He thought the object of *Ghosts* appeared to be, to exalt "free love" and to represent the restrictions of marriage as a tyranny. *Measure for Measure* he denounced as "disfigured by a persistent and exaggerated employment of the sex motive." Such remarks were seized upon gleefully by the Press. The box office was besieged. Miss Baylis thought it disappointing that the Festival should be greeted by the chief representative of the Church of England in Buxton as though its objects were the corruption of public morality. She was content to let the three great plays chosen speak for themselves, but suggested

> the moral of *Measure for Measure* seems to me to be "Judge not that ye be not judged" ... if this play be ... "disfigured by a persistent and exaggerated employment of the sex motive," the same disfigurement appears in the Old Testament and most of the works of St Paul.[9]

Canon Moncrieff was unrepentant. He saw the plays, but saw no reason to change his opinion of them.

A brilliant audience assembled for the first night of *Pygmalion,* the opening play. Just before curtain rise, the theatre was plunged into darkness. The town's electricity supply had failed. Captain F. S. Holmes, manager, torch in hand, went on stage to reassure the audience, whereupon all the lights came up again. And as if to reinforce his message, a black cat made a stately progress along the footlights during the second interval. The play was well received, but Miss Baylis was not entirely satisfied; in her curtain speech, looking beyond the fashionable audience in the crowded stalls and dress circle, she declared

> I don't want to see the gallery looking like this again please. It is nearly empty.[10]

Her words were heeded. The Opera House was packed, night after night, and all three plays were warmly praised.

There were 206 people in the gallery for the final performance of *Pygmalion!* Total attendances over the three weeks were 16,167 and the Festival made a profit of nearly £400. Not only had the town had the pleasure and excitement of seeing fine plays well acted, but visitors had had an especially interesting time - there seemed always to be something going on - and shops, hotels, restaurants and other businesses had all increased their revenue. Press coverage had been massive. That could only be good for the town. There could be few people left in the land who had not heard of Buxton and the Peak District by the end of the Festival. The Old Vic's work had been seen by northern audiences, and the great lady who had toiled at the Old Vic for more than 40 years, and added Sadlers Wells from 1931, Miss Lilian Baylis, had been left in no doubt of everyone's gratitude and regard.

In addition to the plays at the Opera House, the Festival included a British Drama League Summer School at the Playhouse and the Grange, an extensive theatre exhibition in the Pavilion corridors, with a wonderful series of models made by staff and pupils of Buxton College, and a series of lectures and social gatherings where artists and audiences met, talked, ate and danced. Tyrone Guthrie, director of *Pygmalion* and *Measure,* and Esmé Church, director of *Ghosts,* were constantly in demand and most generous with their time and energy. Imposing academics gave lectures, but the most popular of the series was that given by Miss Baylis. She was billed to speak on The Old Vic. Mr G. L. Q. Henriques presided. He introduced her as "one of the most remarkable women of our time":

> Actors and actresses come and go, but the name of Lilian Baylis will be handed down to posterity as that of one of the greatest women of all time in connection with the theatre.
>
> I know you will not misunderstand me when I say I think she is the greatest unmarried mother in the world. (Laughter and applause). All the actors and

---

[8] Daily Dispatch 25 August 1937.
[9] Evening Chronicle 25 August 1937.
[10] Daily Dispatch 31 August 1937.

actresses who have the honour to be invited to play at the Old Vic are her children[11]

Miss Baylis gave what she called "a chat". She told her audience a great deal of the Old Vic's history, particularly of the great enterprise of producing all Shakespeare's plays, *Titus Andronicus* included (although it was left until last because she disliked it so much!). She spoke of enormous financial problems, and expressed gratitude for the help of many famous people. Some of her reminiscences were hilarious. When the Old Vic Company went to Brussels and presented five plays within eight days, King Albert was full of admiration. He wished to tell them how much he had enjoyed *The Tempest,* but could not think of the name Caliban;

> ...and so we had the spectacle of the King, in his magnificent tight fitting uniform, crawling all around the box to show us Caliban. He was a wonderful actor, and made his face quite bestial.[12]

There were loud cheers at the close of the Festival, when the Mayor, Dr W. Shipton, whose casting vote, be it remembered, made the Festival possible, announced that, subject to the approval of the Governors of the Old Vic, the Company would return for a second Festival in Buxton in 1938. Miss Baylis received a "great ovation" when she stepped forward to confirm the Company's promise to return, and to thank the people of Buxton for their goodwill towards the company.

Let R. J. Finnemore have the last word for the 1937 Festival in Buxton:

> What the Festival has demonstrated is that there are thousands of people eager to go to the theatre if they are confident of seeing good acting in plays.[13]

Only two months later, on Thursday 25 November, Miss Baylis died. The national Press carried tributes to her, and so many people crowded St Martin in the Fields church for the memorial service the day after her cremation that Laurence Olivier and the Vanbrugh sisters had to stand in the gallery. St John Ervine, not always her greatest admirer, summed up the source of strength in her work:

> The most obvious fact about this singular woman

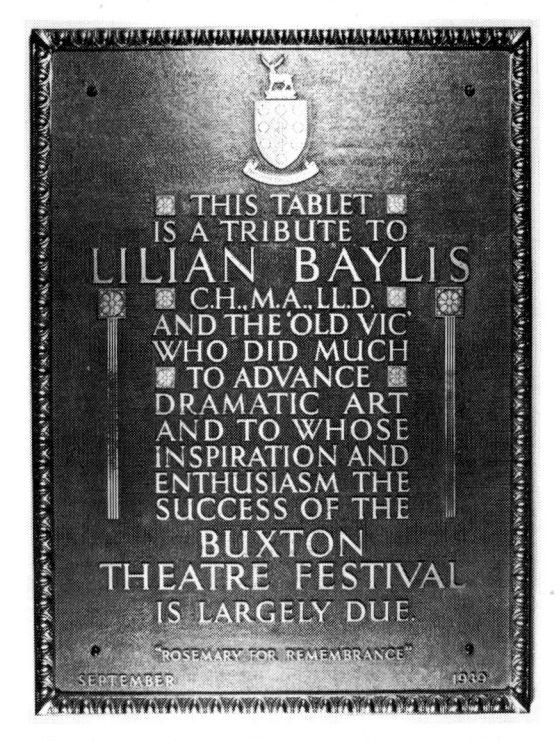

The plaque at the top of the stairs in the foyer of Buxton Opera House, unveiled by Robert Donat in September 1939. "Rosemary for Remembrance" echoes Ophelia's words in Act IV scene 5 of Shakespeare's Hamlet. Miss Baylis gave sprigs of white heather to members of the Old Vic Company on first nights for many years. In 1937, the year of her death, at Buxton and later at the Old Vic, she gave sprigs of rosemary.

was her utter selflessness and her unbounded devotion to her job. The Old Vic was the beginning and the end of her life... She had a single-track mind, the awful concentration of the saint... If she was hard on others she was hard on herself. She did not expect

---

[11] High Peak News 18 September 1937.

[12] ibid.

[13] Daily Dispatch 1 October 1937.

anymore from other people than she expected from Miss Baylis...[14]

Had Miss Baylis read those words, one is tempted to think, she would have added "and Sadlers Wells" in the margin. Buxton honoured her memory. A plaque, unveiled by Robert Donat in 1939, may still be seen at the top of the stairs in the main foyer.

Once again, in 1938, Buxton received valuable pre-Festival publicity. Major Proctor, MP for Accrington, put questions in the Commons to the Minister of Health, Sir Kingsley Wood, to discover whether Buxton Corporation, in undertaking to pay the Old Vic Company £2,125 for salaries, plus all cartage charges, half the cost of lighting and all the cost of advertising and theatre staff for the 1937 Festival, was acting in accordance with the Buxton Corporation Act 1927, whereby no loss may be occasioned to the ratepayers by such promotion of stage plays. He asked what control The Minister exercised to ensure that municipalities made only legitimate use of their powers in providing entertainment. The Minister replied that he had no powers to investigate this matter. The proper form of control would appear to be that of audit, or of action taken by an aggrieved ratepayer. The Manchester Evening News of 4 May 1938 reported Major Proctor's reasons for his attempt to have an official inquiry:

> I am opposed to municipal trading in any form, except where there is a monopoly, as in the case of water and gas. Other trading interferes with the legitimate business of other people. I think it should be checked. It is the advance of Socialism, most insidious and coming in many ways....

Buxton Corporation solved the problem neatly. Alderman F. Hall announced the decision, after private discussion with the Mayor (Mr J. W. Wain) and the Town Clerk (Mr H. C. Hoggett)

> .... we have decided to hand over the running of the Festival to High Peak Entertainments Ltd., who are lessees of the Opera House. As the Opera House is the only place of its kind in the town, we are not in competition with any other enterprise.[15]

Neither Major Proctor nor the Secretary of the Theatrical Managers' Association appears to have been happy about this statement, but announcements of the plays for the forthcoming Festival were soon filling columns in all the papers. The Festival was to run from 29 August to 17 September. The plays were *Hamlet,* Sheridan's *The Rivals* and Pinero's *Trelawney of the Wells. Hamlet,* the title role to be played by a young actor named Alec Guinness, caused most comment. Tyrone Guthrie, now in charge at the Old Vic, announced that the play would be presented in its entirety (almost 4000 lines) and in modern dress. The vicar of Buxton was silent. Almost everyone else commented volubly and at length. Sir Barry Jackson, in his capacity as a Governor of the Old Vic, announced that he was happy to help to organise the Festival (pace GBS!). Mr J. E. Boddington, Manager of the Pavilion Gardens and indefatigible Secretary of the Festival, told the Press that Sir Barry "expressed amazement and pleasure" that there were, under one roof, "two such admirably equipped theatres" as the Opera House (for the plays) and the Playhouse (for the drama school.)

> This happy combination of two theatres under one roof does not exist, of course, in any other resort in the British Isles.[16]

Sir Barry had presented a notable Shakespeare series at the Kingsway in London in the 1920s (the *Hamlet* in 1925) in modern dress. The idea had occurred to him whilst judging a schools drama festival. Team after team had arrived to play scenes from *A Midsummer Night's Dream,* "wrapped in tinsel and towels". Then came a team who could not afford that. They performed the play simply in their ordinary clothes

> and suddenly the play became real and new and immediate. One escaped the atmosphere of a stale ritual, he told the Manchester Guardian. (31 August 1938)

---

[14] The Observer 28 November 1937.
[15] Manchester Evening News 6 May 1938.
[16] A distinction the town has lost, now that the Playhouse has been turned into the Paxton Suite. Restoration to the theatre would be possible, however, should the town ever wish it.

Robert Morley and Diana Wynyard in Shaw's Pygmalion, the play not condemned by the Vicar of Buxton during the Old Vic Festival, Buxton 1937.

Mr Boddington told the *Advertiser* that once again, in the interest of patrons, there would be a morning rendezvous in the Pavilion Gardens at 11.30, when members of the Welcome Committee[17] would be present to introduce patrons to each other, and to members of the Old Vic Company whenever they were free. After each performance, patrons were invited to go to the Pavilion (entrance by their theatre ticket) to meet the performers, to dance to Sammy Greenwood's Band and to patronise the buffet and bar.

The Festival opened with Pinero's *Trelawney of the Wells*:

> Half a dozen mayors[18] jangled into the stalls in their full regalia, and all Buxton's visitors interrupted their taking of the waters to dress in white tie and tails. (Vernon Noble.)

The members of the Company acquitted themselves well: Sophie Stewart, André Morell, Freda Jackson, Anthony Quayle, O. B. Clarence, Alec Guinness, Frank Tickle, Marie Rignold and Andrew Cruickshank, played the somewhat sentimental comedy of a theatre company of the 1860s with obvious delight, and the audience was most receptive. Tyrone Guthrie directed. Next came the Sheridan play, beloved of so many amateur companies, *The Rivals*, directed by Esmé Church. Hermione Hannen played Lydia Languish and Ellen Compton revelled in Mrs Malaprop. A good Sir Lucius O'Trigger was expected from Andrew Cruickshank, and was duly delivered. Alec Guinness "made good fun" as the yokel, Bob Acres. But the production everyone awaited most eagerly, whether to mock or praise, was Shakespeare's *Hamlet*, directed by Tyrone Guthrie and designed by Roger Furse. R. J. Finnemore was in no doubt:

> This complete *Hamlet* in modern dress makes the Buxton Festival an outstanding artistic event. (Daily Dispatch 5 September 38)

[17] The aim of the Welcome Committee: "to create that amiable, sociable and friendly atmosphere which is so indispensable to the success of a festival of this kind."

[18] Ivor Brown described them as "a veritable chain gang" in *The Sketch*.

ALEC GUINNESS.

"Hamlet" Himself.

Why Modern Dress Makes the Part More Strenuous.

Alec Guinness who played the title role in the Old Vic production of Hamlet, Buxton, 1938.

The Times critic declared that *Hamlet* in full

> enables the spectator to move like a swimmer through the succession of waves which compose the narrative and to discover for himself how smoothly each wave hands him over to the next.

One of the surprises of the production was the comparatively short time the full text occupied: three hours and forty minutes acting time. Not everyone was enthusiastic about that. Lionel Hale of the *News Chronicle* complained: he thought it unreasonable

> to force the audience into the theatre at the hungry and unholy hour of 6.40 with a vexatious break for hasty refreshment. A 40 minutes interval is too short for a civilised dinner, and too long for a barbarous sandwich.

Most people appear to have enjoyed the novelty. Hotels and restaurants and the Pavilion Gardens staff co-operated so that the audience could dine within the agreed interval.

An elderly actor, O. B. Clarence (Polonius) accustomed to cut versions of the play, appears to have had some difficulty in remembering the lines usually suppressed, but for the young Alec Guinness[19] the production was a wonderful opportunity which he did not waste. Andrew Cruickshank (Claudius), Anthony Quayle (Laertes), Veronica Turleigh (Gertrude), Hermione Hannen (Ophelia), Frank Tickle (Gravedigger) were all praised repeatedly, and Roger Furse's designs for costume and set made the production splendidly colourful and rich. There had been fears that modern dress would render it drab, but skilful use of court dress, military uniform and evening dress prevented that. Inevitably, in a Tyrone Guthrie production, there was the occasional gimmick. Umbrellas at Ophelia's funeral were approved by most for their "solemn effect". The *Manchester Guardian* critic summed up:

> Remarkable though it may seem, a *Hamlet* that took three hours and forty minutes.... was not wearisome or exhausting, although the Company must indeed have felt, as Mr Guthrie said, that they had bitten off as much as they could chew.

[19] His Hamlet is brilliant, supple and memorable. *(Manchester Guardian).*

The Strand Electric Grand Master lighting board, installed Buxton Opera House 1938 and still in use in 1979.

The Sunlight Gas Panel, removed to the gallery in 1979, is a treasure of Buxton Opera House.

More than one critic praised the very fine Festival "booklet". Copies of these Festival programmes for 1937, 1938 and 1939, still extant, are much prized, and show such praise to be justified.

The *Evening Chronicle* records two very interesting matters from this second Festival: first, the installation of the new Strand Electric lighting switchboard replacing the old gas panel, now preserved outside the gallery, but in 1938 still in situ back stage and, although little over thirty years old then, possibly the only one surviving in position in an English theatre;[20] and second,

> Outside support for the Old Vic Theatre Festival at Buxton has practically guaranteed continuance for the third successive season next year. Local support

is not good, however. About 90 per cent of the audiences come from outside.

O Buxton!

In May 1939 came the welcome announcement that the Old Vic would again present plays at the Buxton Festival. Four plays this time, and for four weeks: 28 August to 23 September. As before, the Buxton Festival would be the prelude to the autumn season at the Old Vic. Tyrone Guthrie was now Director of the Old Vic and Sadlers Wells theatres. He would direct Goldsmith's *The Good*

---

[20] Both switchboards, the gas "Sunlight" and the Strand Electric, were still in position (and the Strand in use!) when the Opera House was restored in 1979, much to the delight of visiting theatre consultants.

81

Natured Man, Miss Esme Church Shaw's *The Devil's Disciple* and Mr Murray Macdonald Shakespeare's *Romeo and Juliet* and Norman Ginsbury's play about the Duchess of Marlborough and Queen Anne, *Viceroy Sarah*. The headlines positively danced when it was announced that Robert Donat, Manchester born film and radio star, would head the company in Buxton. *The Times* headline, "A Galaxy of Talent" seems justified. In company with Mr Donat were Constance Cummings, Marie Ney, Hubert Harben, Stewart Granger, Andre Morell, Andrew Cruickshank, Sonia Dresdel, Max Adrian and others. Not surprisingly, to prevent sieges at the Stage Door, the *Derbyshire Times* records

> The arrangement is being made whereby autograph books may be left at the stage door and collected 48 hours afterwards.

Even so, in a delightful letter to the *Advertiser* in 1979, Mrs Mildred Winterbotham, an usherette in the 1930s, recalls

> I used to sit with Mrs Donat while women chased him (Robert Donat) through the Pavilion Gardens after a matinee.

The Festival opened with *Romeo and Juliet.* Critics were kind: they were content to wait for Mr Donat to adjust to stage acting - he had recently had an enormous film success as the prim, pedantic old schoolmaster, Mr Chips, and the transition to ardent young lover was sudden. Miss Cummings was welcomed. Her American accent troubled some critics. But all were agreed that Stewart Granger made a fine, dark, dashing Tybalt: "a lively cross between a gangster and a Black Prince," wrote Ivor Brown in the *Manchester Guardian.*

Viceroy Sarah followed on Tuesday 29 August. Marie Ney, still vividly remembered as Mrs Alving in *Ghosts* in 1937, was praised for the "graceful vitality" of her playing of Sarah, Duchess of Marlborough. Her quarrel with architect-dramatist Captain Vanbrugh, played by Max Adrian, was delightful. Esmé Church as Queen Anne was a wonderfully "wheezy raddled figure" and Sonia Dresdel as Abigail, who slyly undermines the Duchess's position at court, was outstanding: "the concentrated essence of bitterness and self interest".

References to "the crisis" in several reviews make us look at the dates very carefully. *The Times* headlines "Lure of Robert Donat: Full Houses in spite of Crisis" bring to mind the Ball on the eve of the Battle of Waterloo:

> The most remarkable feature of this year's drama Festival at Buxton is the calm, unattached way in which the public has allowed the interest of the theatre to outweigh the nervous tension of the international situation. At nearly every performance the "House Full" boards have been out. *(The Times)*

A paragraph in the *Caterer and Hotel Keeper* dated 1 September 1939, however, records the "remarkable" number of enquiries from London and other cities to Buxton hotels and boarding houses:

> Buxton is considered one of the safest places in England so far as air raids are concerned and already numbers of people have arrived "just in case"

The third play, Shaw's *The Devil's Disciple,* was successfully launched on Thursday 31 August and all was set for a wonderful, month-long feast, with one more first night still to come, when the blow fell: war was declared on Sunday 3 September. Theatres and cinemas were closed. Mr Boddington immediately put the case "to the proper authorities" that as Buxton was officially a non-vulnerable area, the Opera House and Pavilion Gardens should be re-opened without delay. The Old Vic Company stayed on, rehearsing mornings and afternoons, hoping desperately to be allowed to continue the Festival. By Saturday 9 September, the Home Secretary had authorised re-opening, subject to certain regulations for public safety.[21] A performance of *The Devil's Disciple* was given on that Saturday and a new schedule of performances was drawn up for the remaining Festival period. Most members of the company sat at tables in the Gardens, addressing envelopes to send out notices of the new arrangements: evening performances at 5.30, matinees at 1.45 on Wednesdays, Thursdays, and Saturdays.

---

[21] Most people thought the modifications imposed were reasonable: no names in lights outside theatres etc, theatres and cinemas to be empty by 10pm. Local authorities had discretion to impose other limitations if public safety required them.

Romeo and Juliet: the Old Vic Company at Buxton, September 1939. (From left): Constance Cummings, Juliet; Robert Donat, Romeo; Hubert Harben, Friar Laurence.

The Good Natured Man opened on Monday 11 September, most members of the audience having remembered to bring their gas masks.

> Relief that the Festival had been rescued seemed to lend wings to every actor's art, and there were deliciously comic performances.

So wrote *The Times's* special correspondent.

Instead of returning to London, to the Old Vic, at the end of the Festival, the Company took the plays to Manchester. Before leaving, Robert Donat unveiled the bronze plaque to Lilian Baylis. He spoke of her with great affection and much humour, and concluded with an earnest appeal to Buxton:

> Never let this Festival die. Whatever the future may hold, keep it alive.[22]

Buxton and the Old Vic succeeded in doing that for three more years, no mean feat in war time. In 1940, there were two plays, August 15 to 24: Goldsmith's *She Stoops to Conquer* and G. M. Sierra's *The World is Yours,* with Renee Ascherson, Alec Clunes, Laurence Payne, Esmé Church and Sonia Dresdel in the Company. That year too saw the first Buxton Opera Festival with a visit by the Old Vic's sister-company, Sadlers Wells Opera, 14 to 19 October, with performances of *The Marriage of Figaro* and *La Traviata*. In a foreword to the programme, Tyrone Guthrie expressed regret that from their repertoire of almost thirty operas they could bring only two, and that, although they brought their stars, they came

> unattended by their full compliment of satellites.
>
> C'est la guerre.

Among the Company were Joan Cross, Sumner Austin, John Hargreaves, Ruth Naylor, Roderick Lloyd, Rose Morris and Powell Lloyd. 1941 saw both companies here but for only one week each: the Old Vic Company 11 to 16 August brought Shakespeare's *King John,* and included one matinee performance of the *Medea* by Euripides on the Thursday. Lewis Casson and Sybil Thorndike headed the Company and were superb. From 28 July to 2 August, Sadlers Wells Opera presented *The Beggars Opera* (John Gay and Frederick Austin), *Marriage of Figaro* (Mozart). *Thomas and Sally* (Thomas Arne) in a double bill with *Dido and Aeneas* (Purcell), and *La Traviata* (Verdi). Mrs Winterbotham's letter captures the atmosphere of a performance of *La Traviata*

> ....the only time I have ever seen the Opera House really come into its own. I stood in a box and looked down at the audience. Every seat was occupied. Most of the men were in officer's uniform, but the silence was uncanny. Everyone there was lost in the beauty and sheer perfection of the singers, story and music.

The Sixth Festival, 22 June to 11 July 1942, opened with performances of Laurence Housman's play *Jacob's Ladder* and continued with three Shakespeare plays: *Othello, Merry Wives of Windsor* and *Merchant of Venice*. Principal members of the Company were Rosalind Atkinson, Frederick Valk, Hermione Hannen, Bernard Miles, Freda Jackson and Frank Petley. Programmes (meagre war time issue) included the information:

> These performances are given with the goodwill and assistance of CEMA (Council for the Encouragement of Music and the Arts.) CEMA's policy is "The Best for the Most." CEMA believes that nowhere is this policy better realised than in its specially arranged tours of the Old Vic.

Once again a cruel war brought sad changes to the Opera House. In the long cinema period which ensued, local amateur companies from time to time brought back live theatre for a few nights, and many Buxtonians now alive remember with affection Christmas pantomimes there, but Buxton's "gem" lost its sparkle. Over the years, paint peeled, the roof deteriorated, rain poured in, timbers began to rot. On Thursday 21 October 1976 the *Advertiser* reported that after the end of the BADOS production of *Oklahoma* that week, the Opera House would be closed until the following Spring. It was expected that some urgent work would be carried out, and that careful inspection would be made of the whole structure.

Buxton and High Peak Entertainments Ltd, part of the Hutchinson Leisure Group of Burnley, held the Opera

---

[22] Yorkshire Post 25 September 1939.

House on lease from the High Peak Borough Council:

> For some time the Company have felt that the Opera House is not meeting adquately their requirements of it as a cinema .... the theatre is cold, that it needs substantial refurbishing, and that this is having an effect on attendances to the extent that the availability and choice of films for hire to them is affected.

Since the lease expired in 1981, the Company felt that the short period remaining would not justify their spending money to refurbish the Opera House.

The Council and the Company issued a joint statement, to the effect that they had established a basis for negotiations to continue, and eventually, on Sunday 3 April, the Opera House reopened with the film *King Kong*, to be followed by others, including *Mandingo*:

> Expect all that the motion picture screen has never dared to show before. Expect the truth.

Meanwhile, on a family outing to Buxton, Malcolm Fraser and friends had noticed the words Opera House over an appealing building on the edge of the Pavilion Gardens. The thought of putting on opera in such an attractive place was sufficiently compelling to make him seek out Councillor Ray Walter, Chairman of High Peak Amenities Committee, who arranged for him to see the theatre and who took up his ideas with alacrity. Within a surprisingly short space of time, High Peak Entertainments Ltd had agreed to give up the remaining years of their lease. Enthusiastic Councillors agreed that the theatre should be restored, meetings were held and The Duke of Devonshire, true to Cavendish traditions, generously agreed to help to launch a public appeal for money for restoration. He gave the first £1,000 to start the fund. Press reports soon brought results. Money began to arrive, and letters with donations and offers of help, rolled in. One of the first and most charming of these, dated 21 March 1978, came from Italy:

> Sir,
> I have read with interest Press reports concerning the possibility of establishing an Opera House Foundation in Buxton, under the patronage of His Grace The Duke of Devonshire, and the reports have

Side entrance to the Upper Circle, Buxton Opera House, just before the 1979 restoration began, showing the effects of water ingress.

taken my thoughts back to some 65/70 years ago when as a teenaged child I used to be taken to that lovely spot in the Peak District for the annual summer holidays.

I certainly recollect vividly my first impressions, contrasting the clean, green, quiet atmosphere, with the rather dark one of the environs of Manchester where we then resided, and most of all, my joy at having the opportunity of visiting the Gardens, to which I had a ticket enabling me to enter as though I was the owner! Such a lot of amusements there were, Bowls, Tennis, Croquet, and Boating too, and best of all the Evening Symphony Concerts, where such famous musicians as the Hambourg Brothers, Mischa Elman, and others appeared, and due to them my first notions of music were fostered.

My biggest thrills included visiting the Opera House at matinées, probably without my elders' knowledge,

Inspecting progress (left) during restoration, 1979. (From left): Michael Williams, vice-chairman; Cllr Brenda Tetlow, Mayor; Sir Spencer Le Marchant MP; Cllr Margaret Millican MBE, chairman; Tony Sutton, Arup Associates; the late Sir Graham Page MP; Ros McCoola; David Hincks, Bovis. Right: The Duchess of Gloucester, during her visit to Buxton Opera House in 1978, with Colonel Peter Hilton, Lord Lieutenant of Derbyshire, Cllr Millican and Jeff Clarke, a St Andrews graduate who did much valuable fund-raising and publicity in 1978.

and sometimes being permitted to watch the plays from behind the curtain, and seeing such actors as Martin Harvey in *The Only Way,* and *A Cigarette Makers Romance,* as well as some of Conan Doyle's plays such as *The Speckled Band* which was quite a "shocker".

We were taken to Chatsworth, and Haddon Hall, where I remember being shown a crude wooden cradle where Queen Elizabeth had lain as a baby, it was said. There were long walks to "The Cat and Fiddle", "Goyts Valley", "Solomon's Temple" and "Lover's Leap", and my first sight of the two-deck vehicles known as Charabancs as also the hand-propelled strange Bath-chairs near the Pump Room.

I would indeed be happy to participate in your efforts to collect the requisite funds with which to establish the Foundation, and wish you and the organisers every success. Kindly let me know to whom I should address my contribution, and the correct address.

The contribution arrived: one thousand pounds!

Two boards were formed: Buxton Opera House Trust, chairman Mrs Margaret Millican, vice chairman Michael Williams, and Buxton Festival, chairman David Rigby.

Both Boards bent their energies to raising money, the Trust for restoring the interior of the Opera House (the exterior was to be the responsibility of the owner of the property, High Peak Borough Council), the Festival Board for mounting an Arts Festival. Incredibly restoration began in January 1979, the worst winter for thirty years. Arup Associates were responsible for design, Bovis and others for carrying out the necessary work. Iain Mackintosh and colleagues of Theatre Projects Consultants were closely involved. Derek Sugden, engineer/architect of Arup Associates was leader of the imposing team of experts entrusted with the restoration. He had recently restored Glasgow's Theatre Royal, a nightmare assignment, so that Buxton Opera House, in contrast, must have seemed an uncomplicated operation. He found the theatre very well put together, with well constructed stone walls and a timber structure for the stage tower. There were no structural problems, but, as at Glasgow, an orchestra pit[23] of greater size and depth was needed, necessitating cantilever stage construction and

---

[23] An orchestra player comments: widening orchestra pits is a sinful waste of money, brought about because wind players have taken to loud, modern, large-bore horn, trombone, Heckel bassoon etc. To balance these, more and more string players are added. Then singers complain that orchestras are too loud.

deep excavations which inevitably always seem to coincide with streams, rivers and natural springs.[24]

The essential tasks were: to create an orchestra pit as large as the geometry and acoustic of the auditorium would allow, and to restore the Opera House as near as possible to Matcham's original design.[25]

Very soon, all seating was removed from the stalls, carpets and linoleum were taken up, dust sheets and sheets of plastic were put over seating elsewhere, and a forest of scaffolding, ladders and platforms filled the auditorium from floor to ceiling. Electric wiring was renewed, new positions for stage lighting were provided and "appropriate decorative light fittings" reinstated throughout the House. The famous 1930s "grand master" switchboard was reconditioned, but the possibility of connecting a portable, modern "memory" stage lighting system was made available. The heating system was renewed and provided via the decorative old radiators. The Edwardian ventilation system was reinstated. Another valuable survival, the gas fired "sunburner" in the dome, was dismantled, modified for North Sea gas, cleaned and replaced in working order, thanks to North West Gas. Colour schemes were decided upon, not merely to be true to Press descriptions in 1903, but to harmonise with the curtains, which would be too expensive to replace, and with the carpet, specially woven by Firths, the Brighouse firm who made the original carpet. A piece of the original, three layers down, was discovered in one of the boxes and Firths copied it, bringing a 1907 loom into action again for the purpose. Rather endearingly, the palette for the final scheme of blue, brown, cream, white and gold, came from the wall tiles in the Pit (now the Stalls) which in 1903 ensured "cleanliness and brightness" in that part of the House. The lovely ceiling panels were cleaned, the dressing rooms also. The most complicated work was excavating the orchestra pit: it can now accommodate an orchestra of eighty. A Green Room for the musicians was "invented" over the area where a particularly lively spring formerly gushed to the surface. The original stage structure was left undisturbed: cantilever steel beams

Sir John Betjeman, the late much loved Poet Laureate, beaming upon the Opera House during his visit in 1979.

were introduced to support it. Such marvels are child's play, apparently, to engineer-architects!

Anyone alive and living in Buxton in 1979 must be forgiven for boring later generations with ever more exaggerated accounts of that year's three marvels: the snow (January to May), the restoration of the Opera House (the same months!) and the first International Arts Festival (30 July to 12 August), which marked the re-opening of the restored Opera House, completed on time at a cost of £480,000.

Three marvels certainly; one is tempted to call them miracles. Concerted human endeavour may move mountains, but some supernatural help tends to make the outcome certain.

Some supernatural power was necessary on the first day of the first Festival: Monica Pick-Hieronimi, the soprano, succumbed to tonsilitis at 11 am. At that hour Deborah Cook was in her kitchen near Munich planning luncheon. The telephone rang. At 12 noon she was boarding an aeroplane at Munich airport, still in the same

---

[24] Derek Sugden: Engineering the Restoration pp75-77: *Curtains!!!* edited by Iain Mackintosh and Michael Sell. Published: John Offord (Publications) Ltd. 1982.

[25] The original Pit bench positions and the two gangways showed clearly when all floor covering was removed. Thrilled as I am with the restoration, I do regret that the two gangways were not reinstated. I grieve at the later decision to use the stage box (stage left) for lighting controls. R. McC.

clothes and with no luggage, to be met at Manchester airport by Robert Carsen, assistant producer, and driven to Buxton with police escort, whilst she and Robert discussed set and staging.

Meanwhile, oblivious of possible catastrophe, happy Festival-goers crowded the newly refurbished Art Gallery and Museum at the top of Terrace Road for the official opening of the Art Gallery, and of the Exhibition, *The Lamp of Memory*, a fascinating collection of paintings inspired by the works of Sir Walter Scott, and collected by Dr Catherine Gordon. Ros McCoola's exhibition *Buxton Can Go to Blazes!* showing the history of the Opera House from 1903 to 1979, was in the same building.

The most eagerly-awaited event, was, of course, the first performance of the Festival Opera, directed by Malcolm Fraser, artistic director and "onlie begetter" of the Festival. His vision on that family visit to Buxton only two years earlier was now to be realised with the first performance in the restored opera house of Donizetti's *Lucia di Lammermoor*, based upon the novel *Bride of Lammermoor* by Sir Walter Scott, whose works provided the theme for the entire Festival.

People began to gather in the Square long before curtain up, to watch arrivals, and to discuss, with some horror, the news which by now had percolated, that Monica Pick-Hieronimi could not perform. The large, genial presence of Spencer Le Marchant, MP for High Peak, and an indefatigable benefactor of the Festival, was wonderfully reassuring. Trumpets sounded from the balcony, the much loved patron of both Opera House and Festival, His Grace the Duke of Devonshire, arrived. The Lord Lieutenant of Derbyshire and his lady, Colonel and Mrs Peter Hilton, escorted the guest of honour, Her Royal Highness Princess Alice, Duchess of Gloucester, to the top of the stairs in the Foyer for a brief ceremony: the unveiling of a small bronze plaque commemorating the occasion.

At last the House lights dimmed, Anthony Hose brought the Manchester Camerata to attention, the Overture began. The curtain rose, Roger Butlin's set and Fay Conway's superb costumes lit by Nick Chelton drew gasps of delight. Frank Matcham's jewel of a theatre was

Deborah Cook, who, at only a few hours' notice, sang the title role, in the opening night performance of Donizetti's Lucia di Lammermoor at the first Buxton Festival which marked the reopening of the Opera House, July 30, 1979.

once again the home of artistic endeavour. Malcolm Fraser's production of *Lucia* triumphed over all near-disaster, guided to success by Anthony Hose, music director, the undoubted hero of the night, confronted as he was with a prima donna flown in only a few hours previously, well versed in the usual 'cut' version of the Opera, and other principals and chorus, well rehearsed in the un-cut version which they had prepared for the Festival! How everyone triumphed on that night has passed into history and will become legend. Only the Duke of Wellington's words after his victory at Waterloo seem adequate:

> a damned nice thing - the nearest run thing you ever saw in your life.

Opening scene: Lucia di Lammermoor at Buxton Opera House, 1979.

Malcolm Fraser
Artistic Director, Buxton Festival.

Anthony Hose
Musical Director, Buxton Festival.

Monica Pick-Hieronimi in the role of Lucia. She missed the first two performances, but delighted audiences when she recovered mid-week during the first Buxton Festival, 1979.

Left: Festivity in the air outside the restored Opera House, July 1979.

CHAPTER SEVEN

A Joy for Generations to Come

..... the biggest invasion of Buxton since the Romans arrived to taste the water (*Daily Mail* 31 July 1979).

THAT appeared to be the general view of the first postwar Festival at the Opera House. The event received massive attention in the national and international Press, on radio and on television. The most gratifying aspect of such attention was that the artistic standards achieved were so warmly commended.

"Buxton will become the Glyndebourne of the North" was a favourite remark in 1979. The Arts Minister of the time, the Right Honourable Norman St. John Stevas, an enthusiastic First Nighter, reversed it. He said he hoped that Glyndebourne would become, eventually, the Buxton of the South. Seizing a trumpet, he contributed some silver notes to the fanfare announcing the opening of the Festival. He prophesied that the Opera House would be a joy for generations to come.

It is certainly a joy for the present generation, and it all came about in a remarkably short space of time: less than three years from the time of Malcolm Fraser's visit to Buxton when he noticed those words *Opera House* on a whimsical Edwardian building, and set his mind in a fine frenzy rolling ..... The full story of how it was achieved cannot be detailed here, but it is a stirring tale of the dedicated enthusiastic work of a few. Under the chairmanship of David Rigby, a young Manchester businessman, the Festival caught the interest and support of the many who recognise a good thing when they see it.

The benefits to the town of such an enterprise are enormous, and they will increase as years go by, provided the original intentions of maintaining high artistic standards are not dimmed. Janet Warburton, Administrator of the first two festivals, emphasised the benefits which follow successful festivals. She cited the example of Aldeburgh in East Anglia, a place comparatively few people had heard of until Benjamin Britten established an annual festival there:

Lots of people who came for the Festival took to the place, and go back there at other times of the year.

There is abundant evidence to show that that is what has happened to Buxton. The increased number of visitors to the town, almost throughout the year, testifies to that. An important, self-confessed convert to Buxton is Derek Sugden, leader of the team of experts from Arup Associates responsible for the restoration:

I have realised since I came here that it is probably one of the great towns of Europe. It's partly the buildings, partly the people - you can't separate those two things. It's a very unusual place. (*Morning Telegraph* 21 June 1979.)

Of course! Rodney Milnes, whose interview with a Festival celebrity has become traditional, saw the possibilities from the outset:

Buxton is an ideal festival town. It is small. Everything is in walking distance. The buildings are various and unspoilt, from the eighteenth century Crescent to many Edwardian monsters as lovable as the Opera House. Its former spa status means that there is hotel accommodation in plenty .... The surrounding countryside is majestic. Having got off to such a flying start despite all, Buxton promises to be about the most invigorating thing to have happened to the British festival scene since 1947. (*The Spectator* 11 August 1979.)

A person whose work ensured a "flying start" was Helen O'Neill, Director of Publicity for Glyndebourne, who also directed publicity for the first two Buxton Festivals. Zooming up the motorway in her Aston Martin, she was "an invigorating thing" personified, and yet another Buxton convert:

Breathtakingly beautiful Buxton

sang the bright blue, green and white stickers adorning every envelope leaving the Festival Office and Opera House during her two years. Bill Beresford, a chunky Australian, took over publicity in 1981, and continued the work with fine colonial breeziness, ensuring a steady flow of well-informed visitors.

Lord Harewood, Director of English National Opera, and Lady Harewood, attended the 1979 first night. They continue to support the Festival as years pass. They were among guests who crowded the Octagon for a wonderful party after the first performance. Deborah Cook, gallant substitute soprano, was the person everyone wished to meet - a refreshingly simple figure in the sensible cotton shirt and skirt she had been wearing when she left her Munich kitchen so abruptly that morning. "Tell me where I am," she asked. "I know I'm somewhere in the north of England. Where am I in relation to Leeds? I've worked there, so I know where that is."

The first fireworks exploded at midnight. If Roman invaders of Buxton conducted orgies, they could never have been so unaffectedly joyous. The long-quiet Square and Crescent provided a solid background for all the Festival fun and hilarity. They do so each year. They seem to be especially enduring on Festival Last Nights, when people crowd into the Square, long before the last performance ends. Bands play, a good-humoured torchlight procession meanders through the town, increasingly festive as the Crescent is reached. People dance and sing, late diners stroll down from the Palace and Leewood Hotels or along from the Old Hall or St. Ann's Hotels, to join the throng. The party continues, sometimes uproariously, to a late hour, ending with a mammoth barbecue near the George.

All the town's a stage. It is a constant pleasure to see how readily the old buildings, squares, terraces, gardens and slopes lend themselves as back drops for spontaneous "happenings," most of them organised by Sheila Barker, the Fringe Secretary. She and her committee ensure abundant colour and variety, and run a very useful Information Desk in the Pavilion, to help visitors to plan their time and programme. Already the Buxton Fringe rivals Edinburgh's. In Royal Wedding year, 1981, Earl Spencer was plainly fascinated by the al fresco music, dancing, talking and clowning proceeding simultaneously along the promenade and elsewhere. He wandered happily about, camera always ready. Some results are to be seen in the beautiful book, *The Spencers on Spas* which he and Countess Spencer produced in 1983. They came over from Chatsworth with the Duke of Devonshire for the 1981 first night. There were cheers when the now familiar Father-of-the-Bride stepped onto the forecourt. That year, the Lord Lieutenant of Derbyshire and his lady, Colonel and Mrs Peter Hilton, arrived by horse-drawn carriage, a charming reminder of 1903 when almost everyone came by horse drawn conveyance of some kind.

What a joy it is, to have such a focus to attract so many people to the town! Famous faces abound, with a goodly number of politicians, actors, musicians and critics regularly sighted. Two who gave especial pleasure were the Right Honourable George Thomas, Speaker of the House of Commons, now Lord Tonypandy, and Sir Geraint Evans, who ended his magnificent career in opera with farewell performances at Covent Garden in 1984. The annual Granada Literary Luncheon brings famous writers and "best sellers" to the town, and subsequent television programmes help to make the joys of Buxton and its Festival better known.

Foreign visitors come in increasing numbers. The Kodaly Festival, 1982, attracted many Hungarians, and gave them and us, the pleasure of seeing and hearing the composer's widow, Madame Kodaly. The Manchester Camerata, the Festival orchestra since the outset, provided a most appealing occasion in 1983: the orchestra had performed at the festival in Rasiguères, in France, started a few years ago by Moura Lympany. The Camerata invited the villagers of Rasiguères to Buxton. They brought kilos and kilos of snails which they roasted at a glorious party on the terrace of the Palace Hotel, serving them with their local bread, wine and deliciously dressed salads.

Disasters still fall from time to time. The worst within the last five years were the narrowly-averted financial collapse of 1980 and the destruction of the Pavilion lounge, bar, kitchens and restaurant by fire early on a

Sir Spencer Le Marchant, former MP for High Peak (left), a great benefactor of Buxton Festival, with Lord Tonypandy, then the Rt Hon George Thomas, Speaker of the House of Commons.

Christopher Barron
General Manager, Buxton Opera House and Festival.

David Hunter
Chairman, Buxton Festival.

June morning in 1983. The fire raged perilously closely to the Opera House. Firemen kept hoses playing on the west wall to diminish the effect of the terrifying heat generated. Maurice Roberts, Pavilion Gardens General Manager, and his staff, were conducting business almost as usual within a week, but a much-regretted result, owing to lack of space, was the cancellation of *Curtains!!!,* a most informative and imaginative theatre exhibition mounted by Iain Mackintosh and a committee formed for the project. The exhibition showed surviving pre-1914 theatres and music halls of Great Britain, whether in use or not. Buxton Opera House, very much in use, featured prominently.

The gods were kind; the Opera House escaped destruction by fire. It came dangerously close to destruction by finance during the 1980 Festival, the most ambitious Festival until 1984. Two operas were mounted, each with full orchestra and chorus, and thrilling stars. Thomas Allen, England's best baritone, sang the title role in *Hamlet,* the opera by the French composer Ambroise Thomas, directed by Malcolm Fraser; Philip Langridge and Ann Murray were the witty, exciting principals in the Berlioz opera *Beatrice and Benedict,* adapted from Shakespeare's *Much Ado About Nothing,* and directed by Ronald Eyre, well-known for his distinguished work on television and with major theatre companies, but making his debut, brilliantly, in opera direction, with this production at Buxton. The 1980 programme details the richness and variety of music, art, films, lectures and other items in addition to the two operas of this Festival, the whole based upon the theme *Shakespeare,* and with particular reference to the work of Berlioz. Geoffrey Ashton, Librarian of the Garrick Club, mounted a memorable exhibition, *Shakespeare's Heroines,* which was much praised and enjoyed. Quite suddenly, in the second week, disturbing rumours were heard that there would not be enough money to pay artists' salaries. There was a flurry of meetings and the crisis passed, but the repercussions were felt for some time. A strict financial policy was formulated and retrenchment was to be the watch word.

David Hunter became Chairman of the Festival Board at this difficult time. He had to lay down a new policy and attract sponsors in increasing numbers if the deficit were to be reduced and the Festival to continue. By 1982 a small surplus was achieved; by 1983 the Festival made a

Thomas Allen and Christine Barbaux in Hamlet, Buxton Festival 1980.

profit of more than £5,000. Buxton owes a great deal to David Hunter, to the Festival Board, and to the many generous sponsors, whose names should be written in gold, for saving the Festival and guiding it to the present calm seas and prosperous voyage.

Who can forget the two Spring opera seasons at Buxton? In spite of the name, *Opera House,* the theatre rarely has more than the two Festival weeks of opera in a year, so that a week of opera in Spring 1980, and two weeks in Spring 1981, appealed greatly to opera lovers. The first burst upon a delighted High Peak region in March 1980, when Scottish Opera, stranded, homeless at the sudden closure of the Grand Theatre, Wolverhampton, in February, ran to Buxton for shelter and gave four stirring performances to full houses: two of *The Bartered Bride*, two of *Rigoletto*. The following year, Scottish Opera returned for a week in Spring, followed by a week by English National Opera North.

There have been many adverse criticisms of the choice of operas for the Festivals. Every year at the press release, one boring female journalist is heard declaring that the choice should be of "popular" operas: Carmen, La Bohème, La Traviata ... Fortunately Malcolm Fraser and Anthony Hose remain true to their original policy: each Festival is thematic and each includes, as far as possible, works which are rarely, or not previously, performed. This enriches everyone's experience and plainly encourages opera "buffs" to come to Buxton to hear works not available elsewhere. There has been commendable variety in themes and operas:-

1979   Sir Walter Scott
        Donizetti: *Lucia di Lammermoor*
1980   Shakespeare
        Thomas: *Hamlet*
        Berlioz: *Beatrice and Benedict*
1981   David Garrick
        Cimarosa: *The Secret Marriage*
1982   Zoltán Kodály
        Kodály: *Háry János*
1983   Giovanni Boccaccio - *The Decameron*
        Vivaldi: *Griselda*
        Gounod: *La Colombe*
1984   The Greek Revival
        Cherubini: *Medea*
        Cavalli: *Jason*

A popular element in each Festival which has appealed to Buxtonians and ensured their wholehearted co-operation and involvement is the annual Children's Opera. A large number of local children take part each year, with huge enjoyment. The first six were:

1979 Peter Maxwell Davies: *The Two Fiddlers*
1980 Peter Maxwell Davies: *Cinderella*
1981 Benjamin Britten: *Let's Make an Opera*
1982 Charles Strouse: *Nightingale*
1983 Herbert Chappell: *James and the Giant Peach*
1984 Norman Kay: *Robin Hood*

The year 1983 was crowned with success. All three operas were taken to Sadlers Wells and enthusiastically received. *James and the Giant Peach* won the British Theatre

Sir Geraint Evans, who gave a master class in 1982.

Rosalind Plowright, who sang Medea, Buxton Festival 1984.

Ann Murray and Philip Langridge in the title roles: Beatrice and Benedict, Buxton Festival 1980.

Members of the award-winning Buxton Festival Children's Opera Company's James and the Giant Peach at Sadlers Wells Theatre, London, during triumphant performances there in September 1983.

Association's Drama Award for the best children's production in 1983 - a delightful reward for a hard-working company.

The degree of local involvement in both theatre and Festival has increased steadily with the years. The children's operas undoubtedly aroused the interest of local schools and hence of the parents and friends of the children involved. An amazing number of people will be found helping each year. The Opera House, for example, has never had to pay wages to front-of-house staff. From the very outset, Bob Burrows has acted as honorary house manager, Nora, his wife, has organised the teams of stewards and bar attendants who give their services free, night after night, throughout the year, Bob Mulholland has edited the newsletter, *On Stage*, since January 1980, and volunteers have helped to distribute copies so that people may be kept informed of the great variety of entertainment the Opera House offers each year: plays, musicals, ballet, concerts, (the Hallé every September!) recitals, choirs, brass bands, gang shows, jazz groups, country and western groups, well-known comedians and so on - the list seems endless. Everyone must surely find some items of entertainment within a year. Many people involve themselves in fund raising activities for the theatre or the Festival also, ranging from simple coffee mornings, *At Homes* in the Opera House, gatherings of various kinds in stately homes and elsewhere. In 1980 a Festival Society was formed under the chairmanship of Mr Henry Hartley, the much respected lawyer who at earlier times saved Buxton's railway from Dr. Beeching's axe and led the battle, culminating in victory in the House of Lords, to prevent a casino being established in the Pavilion. He was succeeded as chairman by Mr. Martin Brooke-Taylor, another of the town's lawyers, in 1982. Howard Barker is the Society's indefatigable secretary. The Festival Society has raised considerable sums over the years to help to finance the Festival. A sum of £2,000 from the splendid Fashion Show at Chatsworth in 1982 by Mrs Diana Bates and her helpers was a particularly fine effort. But there have been many others, and both organisations, theatre and Festival, continue to welcome (and need!) such support. An interesting venture to raise money for the theatre, and to draw in audiences from all over the High Peak region, is the Willoughby Luncheon Club. This club, named after John and Arthur Willoughby, founder and first manager of the Opera House in 1903, exists for people who live outside the town. In its first year it raised over £1,000 for the upkeep of the theatre, and brought new friends in from outlying areas.

Gerald Larner wrote in *The Guardian* in 1979:

> After the Festival, Buxton sinks back into its small town way of life, but the restored Opera House will still be there as a community asset.

Not everyone, even yet, realises what an enormous asset the Opera House is to the region, if properly used and organised. After the Festival's financial crisis of 1980, High Peak Borough Council, which had guaranteed the Festival against loss, then showed a more lively interest in the Opera House itself. The stolid persistence of the chairman of the Opera House Trust, Mrs. Margaret Millican, whose M.B.E. was well and truly earned, the legal awareness of the vice-chairman, Mr. Michael Williams, and the dedication of members of the Opera House Board ensured survival of the theatre.

In December 1983 a most important step was taken: High Peak Borough Council accepted more responsibility, in effect, for helping to keep the Opera House solvent. The Opera House Board was reconstituted: some board members who had served since the enterprise began and had given most valuable service and support now stood down, and a smaller board was constituted with a majority of Council members. This is a praiseworthy development: it means that the local council accepts responsibility for the community's theatre.

Christopher Barron, appointed General Manager in 1981, has worked hard, with his assistant Jane Herbert, and other members of staff, to extend what the theatre can offer. A pleasing development was the inauguration of an assisted transport scheme to make theatre going (the Opera House habit!) possible from all parts of the region. A leaflet obtainable from the theatre gives details of this ingenious scheme. Plans to involve teachers and pupils are very much Mr. Barron's concern. This is to be applauded for many reasons, not least that it is educating audiences of the future.

With such positive, hopeful developments in the High Peak area, the next step must be to convince Derbyshire County Council that Buxton Opera House and Buxton Festival are vital assets for the whole County of Derbyshire. If encouraged and assisted, they will help to generate the funds for housing and the other services which rightly preoccupy the minds of councillors.

Ars longa, vita brevis .... The Opera House survives, and triumphs, a welcoming home for the Festival and much else. David Garrick, an 18th century actor all the world reveres, whose death, Dr. Johnson said, eclipsed the gaiety of nations, knew and loved Buxton:

> I stayed about five days and never was more merry or in higher spirits in my life.

Gentle readers, please copy! Come to Buxton, the best town in Europe, stay at least five days, and be merry.

UPPER CIRCLE   DRESS CI